MW01225650

OTHER TITLES IN THE CODENOTES SERIES

CodeNotes for J2EE: EJB, JDBC, JSP, and Servlets

CodeNotes for XML

CodeNotes for .NET

CodeNotes for Java: Intermediate and Advanced Language Features

CodeNotes for Web-Based UI

CodeNotes® for VB.NET

Edited by GREGORY BRILL

CodeNotes®
for VB.NET

RANDOM
HOUSE

NEW YORK

Copyright © 2001 by Infusion Development Corporation

All rights reserved under International and Pan-American Copyright Conventions. Published in the United States by Random House, Inc., New York, and simultaneously in Canada by Random House of Canada Limited, Toronto.

RANDOM HOUSE TRADE PAPERBACKS and colophon are trademarks of Random House, Inc.

CodeNotes® is a registered trademark of Infusion Development Corporation.

Access, ActiveX, Authenticode, ClearType, DirectX, FrontPage, Internet Explorer, JScript.NET, Microsoft, MS-DOS, MSDN, Outlook, PowerPoint, SQL Server, Visual Basic, Visual Basic.NET, VBScript, Visual C#.NET, Visual C++, Visual C++.NET, Visual InterDev, Visual Studio, Visual Studio.NET, Win32, Win64, Windows, Windows 95, Windows 98, Windows 2000, Windows Me, Windows NT, Windows XP, are registered trademarks or trademarks of Microsoft Corporation in the United States and/or other countries.

Java and JavaServer Pages are trademarks or registered trademarks of Sun Microsystems, Inc., in the U.S. and other countries

Library of Congress cataloging-in-publication data is available.

ISBN 0-8129-9215-6

Website address: www.atrandom.com

24689753

First Edition

Using CodeNotes

PHILOSOPHY

The CodeNotes philosophy is that the core concepts of any technology can be presented succinctly. Building from many years of consulting and training experience, the CodeNotes series is designed to make you productive in a technology in as short a time as possible.

CODENOTES POINTERS

Throughout the book, you will encounter CodeNotes Pointers (e.g., ⟨CN⟩VB010010). These pointers are links to additional content available online at the CodeNotes website. To use a CodeNotes pointer, simply point a web browser to www.codenotes.com and enter the pointer number. The website will direct you to an article or an example that provides additional information about the topic.

CODENOTES STYLE

The CodeNotes series follows certain style guidelines:

- Code objects and code keywords are highlighted using a special font. For example, `System.Object`.

- Code blocks, screen output, and command lines are placed in individual blocks with a special font:

```
//This is an example code block
```

WHAT YOU NEED TO KNOW BEFORE CONTINUING

The .NET Framework encompasses concepts ranging from distributed computing to database access to public key cryptography. Because the topics are so varied, the CodeNotes format is compressed and certain background information has been omitted. However, a significant number of examples and background articles can be found on the CodeNotes website.

About the Authors

SHELDON FERNANDEZ is a senior developer at Infusion Development Canada in Toronto, Ontario. He has developed software for Silicon Valley startups, as well as for financial and medical firms in the United States and Canada. He has worked with Microsoft technology for many years, from his very first QuickBasic compiler to latest suite of .NET development tools. Sheldon, who possesses a computer engineering degree from the University of Waterloo, was also the chief researcher for *Applying COM+,* a definitive work on Microsoft's enterprise component technology.

ALIM SOMANI is a senior developer and trainer at Infusion Development Canada. He has lived, traveled, and developed software throughout North America and Europe. He has written software systems for the financial, retail, and medical industries. He holds a degree in electrical engineering from the University of Waterloo and currently resides in Toronto, Ontario.

GREGORY BRILL is president of Infusion Development Corporation, a firm specializing in architecting global-securities-trading and analytic systems for several of the world's largest investment banks in the United States and Tokyo. He has written articles for *C++ Users Journal,* and he is the author of *Applying COM+.* He lives in New York City.

More information about the authors and Infusion Development Corporation can be found at www.infusiondev.com/codenotes.

Acknowledgments

First, thanks to John Gomez who saw the potential of the CodeNotes idea before anyone else and introduced me to Random House. Without John, there would be no CodeNotes. I'd also like to thank Annik La-Farge, who fearlessly championed the series and whose creativity, enthusiasm, and publishing savvy has been instrumental in its creation. Thank you to Mary Bahr, our unflappable editor, who paved the way and crafted the marketing. Thank you to Ann Godoff, whose strength, decisiveness, and wisdom gave CodeNotes just the momentum it needed. And, of course, the production, sales, and business teams at Random House, with particular thanks to Howard Weill, Jean Cody, and Richard Elman.

On the Infusion Development side, thank you to Sheldon Fernandez and Alim Somani, the writers of this CodeNotes title. They are a fantastic team and delivered a great book. Thank you to Derek Barnes for doing a super job on the first round of technical reviews and edits and to Rob McGovern for all of his feedback and suggestions. Thank you also to the CodeNotes reviewers, who gave us invaluable feedback and suggestions on our early drafts. And thank you to the entire cast and crew of Infusion Development Corporation, who have supported and encouraged this venture throughout, with special thanks to Irene Wilk-Dominique, Jessica Pollack, and DeBorah Johnson who helped administrate and manage so much. Here it is, CodeNotes . . . as we envisioned it.

—Gregory Brill

Contents

CodeNotes® for VB.NET

Chapter 1

———

VB.NET AND THE .NET FRAMEWORK

Visual Basic is a creature that must evolve. Since its inception 10 years ago, each new version of the product has boasted additional capabilities to adapt to new technologies and paradigms. Visual Basic 5, for example, allowed developers to create ActiveX controls when Microsoft was attempting to foster the ActiveX proprietary technology. Visual Basic 6 introduced the Web Class Designer that greatly simplified the deployment of web applications using Dynamic HTML. VB.NET continues the evolutionary trend, but on a much grander scale. It is fair to say that VB.NET (what was once thought of as VB7) represents the most fundamental change in the Visual Basic language ever. Several aspects of the product that have remained consistent since VB's original release are different under VB.NET:

- The Visual Basic IDE is now integrated with VS.NET, Microsoft's next version of Visual Studio. This means that VB now shares its design environment with other Microsoft languages such as Visual C++.
- The Visual Basic Forms engine that drove form design in previous versions of VB has been replaced with Windows Forms, the new way to design desktop GUIs. Although Windows Forms stil! employs the same intuitive approach to application design (whereby one *paints* applications by dragging and dropping controls onto a form), it exposes many details abstracted in previous versions of VB.

- VB.NET has its own command-line compiler (called vbc.exe), allowing you to compile applications outside the Visual Basic environment. You can, for example, write VB source code using a text editor such as Notepad and then compile the source file from the command prompt.

In addition to these noteworthy changes, the language's syntax has been modified significantly. Array bounds, parameter passing, and control properties, for example, all behave differently under VB.NET. New features such as C++ try/catch error handling routines, multithreading, and object-oriented concepts such as inheritance have been added to the language. Microsoft has also removed numerous elements from the VB syntax. Among others, Variant, GoSub, IsNull, and IsMissing have all been retired.

Although each new version of a product raises compatibility issues, the magnitude of changes in VB.NET makes migration a prime concern for many developers. In Chapter 3, we investigate VB.NET's syntax changes in detail, as well as the Upgrade Wizard, which is designed to assist developers porting VB6 code to VB.NET.

The .NET Framework

To understand VB.NET, you must understand its new ecological niche—the .NET Framework. Simply put, .NET is Microsoft's new strategy for the development and deployment of software. Depending on your interests and development background, you may already have a number of ideas about what exactly .NET is. As we will see in these CodeNotes,

- .NET fundamentally changes the way applications execute under the Windows operating system.
- With .NET, Microsoft is, in effect, abandoning its traditional stance, one that favors compiled components, and is embracing interpreted technology (similar in many ways to the Java paradigm).
- In addition to radically overhauling Visual Basic, .NET also brings about significant changes to Visual C++ and introduces a new language called C# (pronounced "C-sharp").
- .NET is built from the ground up with the Internet in mind, embracing open Internet standards such as XML and HTTP. XML is also used throughout the framework as both a messaging instrument and for configuration files.

These are all noteworthy features of .NET, or more accurately the .NET Framework, which consists of the platform and tools needed to develop and deploy .NET applications.

A UNIVERSAL RUNTIME

To effectively write programs in VB.NET, you must understand two .NET entities: the Common Language Runtime (CLR) and the Base Class Libraries (BCL). If you have worked with Visual Basic 6 before, you have in fact already used lesser versions of both entities. To understand how, let us consider the VB6 Runtime file (MSVBVM60.DLL) that must accompany every VB6 application you deploy.

Although distributing the 1.4-megabyte runtime file with your VB6 applications is annoying, it is essential for two reasons:

1. The VB Runtime provides services such as automatic memory management, string allocation/deallocation, and saftey checking on code. If, for example, your VB code tries to reference an array outside its boundaries, the VB Runtime steps in and informs you that an illegal operation is being performed. This is in contrast to languages such as C and C++, where memory access is not monitored, resulting in potentially catastrophic failures if code misbehaves. And, unlike C and C++, the VB Runtime will automatically clean up after you, destroying objects and variables once they go out of scope.

2. The VB Runtime also houses intrinsic VB functions such as `MsgBox`, `Ubound`, and `InStr`. For years, VB developers have routinely used such functions for string manipulation, type conversion, and user input. The code for these functions is contained in the VB Runtime. When you call `Mid()` to extract a substring from a string, you are really calling a function in the VB Runtime that performs the work. Without the VB Runtime, a VB application would be reduced to a meaningless collection of function calls.

From these two observations, it can be said that a Visual Basic 6 application runs *within* the VB Runtime. In fact, the name of the runtime file is indicative of this very purpose: MSVBVM stands for **M**icro**S**oft **V**isual **B**asic **V**irtual **M**achine. With VB.NET, the VB Runtime has grown into two separate and larger entities: the Common Language Runtime and the Base Class Libraries.

The Common Language Runtime

The Common Language Runtime (CLR) is the execution environment for all programs in the .NET Framework. The CLR is similar to a Java Virtual Machine (VM), which interprets bytecode and executes it on the fly. Instead of interpreting Java bytecode, however, the CLR reads Microsoft Intermediate Language (IL) code that is produced by the VB.NET compiler. Like the VB Runtime, the CLR scrutinizes code before it executes to ensure that it stays within its designated boundaries. The CLR also performs a sophisticated type of memory management called *garbage collection,* which we examine in Chapter 6.

Thus, applications written in VB.NET no longer run within the VB Runtime but execute inside the CLR. Code that runs inside the CLR is referred to as *managed code.* Code that executes outside its boundaries (such as that produced by VB6), is called *unmanaged code.* As its name suggests, the *Common* Language Runtime offers its services not only to VB.NET, but to any compiler capable of producing IL code. Think of the CLR as an improved and enlarged version of the VB Runtime, which is now accessible from any .NET language.

The Base Class Libraries

Built-in VB functions such as LBound and UCase are now contained in the Base Class Libraries (BCL), which are prewritten services that clients can use. It helps if you think of LBound and UCase not as VB-specific functions, but as services that were offered to your program by the VB Runtime. In this sense, the Base Class Libraries contain services that form the building blocks for applications in the .NET Framework. We will see how to call these functions in the upcoming example.

In addition to containing functions that were previously intrinsic members of the VB syntax, the BCL contains hundreds of other classes and functions for operations such as File IO, Remote Messaging, and other technologies you may have used in the past (ADO, for example).

The Base Class Libraries (which are automatically copied to your system when you install the .NET Framework, as shown in Chapter 2), exist as language-independent IL code. This means that they are accessible not only from VB.NET, but from any .NET language. Although we will call the Base Class Libraries from VB.NET throughout these Code-Notes, realize that we could do the same with C# or C++. Readers familiar with Java can think of the BCL as analogous to the Java Class Libraries.

MOVING TO VB.NET

The challenges for VB developers migrating to the .NET Framework are fourfold:

1. You must familiarize yourself with the BCL to use functions that were previously intrinsic members of the VB language. Initially, this can be frustrating, as many functions and classes in the BCL behave differently than their VB counterparts. Nevertheless, understanding the BCL is worthwhile, as it contains hundreds of services that previous versions of VB did not expose (classes for threading, linked lists, sophisticated graphics, etc.).
2. You must account for the numerous syntax changes in VB.NET. For example, the default way in which procedure parameters are passed is by value (`ByVal`), not by reference (`ByRef`).
3. You must learn Windows Forms, the new way to design desktop GUIs in the .NET Framework.
4. You must concern yourself with details that previous versions of Visual Basic usually abstracted (concepts such as threading and component versioning).

THE BOOK'S CONTENTS

In this chapter we examine the fundamentals of VB.NET and the .NET Framework.

Chapter 2 provides brief installation instructions. Because .NET was still in beta release at the time of writing, these instructions may be out of date, and readers are encouraged to consult the online instructions at ⟨CN⟩VB020001.

The many new syntax changes from VB6 to VB.NET are covered in Chapter 3. This chapter discusses the removal of `Variant`, changes to class properties characteristics, and the new way to trap errors in VB.NET using structured exception handling. Chapter 3 also illustrates the VB.NET Upgrade Wizard that assists in porting VB6 code to the .NET Framework.

VB.NET includes two new features that developers have been longing for—true class inheritance and threading. Both of these powerful features are investigated in Chapter 4.

The .NET Framework not only changes Visual Basic, but alters fundamental aspects of component distribution and deployment. As shown in Chapter 5, the DLLs and EXEs produced by VB.NET are not the same as those produced by VB6 but are a new type of .NET component called an *Assembly.*

Chapter 6 examines the new language features in the .NET Framework and VB.NET's new event structure. Topics in this chapter include *attributes,* which are nonprogrammatic code statements that can be used to influence application behavior, and *delegates,* the new type-safe callback mechanism in the managed environment. *Garbage collection,* the new way memory is managed in VB.NET, is also investigated, as is *reflection,* the ability to ascertain type information about an application at runtime.

Windows Forms, the subject of Chapter 7, is the new way to construct desktop GUI applications for the Windows environment. Windows Forms is a significant departure from the VB Forms engine that fueled application design in previous versions of VB.

The .NET Framework does not preclude the use of traditional ActiveX controls and components that were used in VB6. Mechanisms exist to call these unmanaged components (those that do not run within the CLR) from VB.NET. Such mechanisms are investigated in Chapter 8.

The final chapter of *CodeNotes for VB.NET* surveys some of the new services in the .NET Framework: ADO.NET, the new data access model in .NET framework; ASP.NET, Microsoft's new-generation Active Server Page (ASP) Framework for developing robust web applications; and Web Services, which allow components to interact via open Internet standards such as XML and HTTP.

The following Core Concepts section defines some of the terminology used throughout this book.

Core Concepts

Visual Studio.NET

Producing .NET applications and components requires a compiler that translates source code into IL code. VS.NET, Microsoft's new version of Visual Studio, contains three such compilers: VB.NET, C#, and managed C++. All three languages share the same design environment—you can develop applications in both C# and VB.NET without having to switch IDEs. In addition to the IDE, VS.NET contains a large assortment of command-line utilities. Some of these utilities are directly incorporated into the development environment, whereas others are stand-alone. We will examine some of these utilities throughout this book.

Development is rarely an individual task. More often than not, a project is a cooperative effort that spans multiple products and individuals. Intermixing languages is likely to become commonplace with .NET, given the language neutrality of the CLR. In Chapter 5, we show how a class written in C# can be inherited and extended easily in VB.NET. Thus, while you do not need to understand either C# or managed C++ to write applications in VB.NET, practical situations may arise when a working knowledge of either language is beneficial. To this end, we now briefly discuss VS.NET's two other languages.

Managed C++

Unlike Visual Basic, C++ does not clean up after the developer. If you allocate memory in C++, the runtime does not ensure that memory is properly released. As a result, C++ developers have long been responsible for managing memory themselves. In addition, C++ allows the use of low-level memory manipulation techniques such as pointers and un-bounded arrays. Although such latitudes can be dangerous if incorrectly used, they are invaluable for computationally intense operations such as image manipulation and numerical calculations.

Moving C++ to the CLR is problematic because of two competing principles:

1. The latitude that C++ gives to developers (direct memory access using pointers, manual memory management, etc.)
2. The CLR's responsibilities of automatic memory management (garbage collection) and code sanity checks (which are difficult to perform given a pointer-ridden language like C++)

Managed C++ is a set of extensions added to the C++ language that enables it to run within the CLR. The most notable extension is the introduction of "managed types," which shift the burden of memory management from the C++ programmer onto the CLR. Placing the __gc extension in front of the declaration of a class, for example, allows instances of the class to be garbage-collected. Another extension is that of managed arrays, which allows these data structures to be managed by the CLR. Managed exception handling is another amendment, which differs from C++ exception handling in both syntax and behavior. Additional information on managed C++ can be found at ☞VB010001.

C#

C# (pronounced "C-sharp") is a new language that Microsoft has touted as a simplified version of C and C++. In this respect, C# is very much like Java, eliminating some of the more complex features of C++ such as pointers and unbounded arrays. Like Java and C++, C# is an object-oriented (OO) language and contains expected OO features such as inheritance, polymorphism, and interfaces (concepts covered in Chapter 4).

As of this writing C# can be used only to produce managed code (i.e., it cannot be used to write code that executes outside the CLR). In this sense, C# can be considered the intrinsic language of the .NET Framework, as it was developed solely for the managed environment. This is in contrast to both C++ and Visual Basic, which had to evolve into their .NET manifestations. It is worthwhile to at least familiarize yourself with C#, since a large portion of .NET sample code on both the Internet and the MSDN is written in C#.

Namespaces

In previous versions of Visual Basic, intrinsic functions such as MsgBox and Mid were globally accessible—you simply used them from your applications without worrying about where they came from. Because the Base Class Libraries contain hundreds of classes and functions, there must be some manner in which to organize them. This is accomplished using namespaces.

Namespaces provide a scope (or container) in which types are defined. Several core BCL classes, for example, are found in the System namespace. If the BCL contained a function called Foo(), for example, you would have to *qualify* it using the System namespace:

```
System.Foo()
```

Namespaces can also be nested. The System.IO namespace, for example, contains a number of classes for I/O operations, whereas System.Collections contains classes for common data structures such as arrays. It is tedious to always have to qualify a BCL class when you use it. Can you imagine writing System.Collections.ArrayList every time you wanted to use the ArrayList class? For this reason, VB.NET allows you to implicitly reference a namespace using the Imports keyword:

```
Imports System
Imports System.Collections

Foo()
ArrayList.Add(30)
```

Because of the two Imports statements, we don't have to write the more verbose code:

```
System.Foo()
System.ArrayList.Add(30)
```

As you can see, implicitly referencing namespaces can save you a lot of typing and make your code easier to read (in the second example in this chapter, we will see that the IDE can automate namespace referencing). You will use namespaces throughout the .NET framework to accomplish the following:

1. Access the BCL classes
2. Access custom classes authored by other developers
3. Provide a namespace for your own classes to avoid naming conflicts with classes not authored by yourself

We will use namespaces throughout this book as we develop our own .NET components.

Common Type System

If you understand the `Variant` data type, you understand the Common Type System (CTS). In VB6, a `Variant` encapsulates all the allowable types in the language (`string`, `int`, `double`, etc). This is all the Common Type System is—a definition of all the permissible types in the .NET Framework. Like a `Variant`, the CTS includes types such as strings and integers, as well as some additional types not found in VB6, such as decimals and chars.

The important thing to understand about the CTS is that it applies not only to VB.NET, but to *all* languages in the .NET Framework. This means that VB.NET, C#, and managed C++ (as well as any future .NET languages) all agree on the types they can use and the representation of those types. As we see in Chapter 5, this facilitates the seamless interoperability between languages in the .NET Framework.

Variants in VB.NET?

In Visual Basic 6, if you were unsure about the contents of a variable, you could have always made it a `Variant`. A popular practice was to have a function return a `Variant` when its return value was not known at design time.

With VB.NET, the `Variant` has been supplanted with the `Object` type found in the `System` namespace. All types in the .NET Framework are derivatives of `Object`. For now, think of an `Object` and `Variant` as equivalent—no matter what its contents, a variable is always an `Object`.

COM

Microsoft's Component Object Model (COM) is the underlying architecture behind VB6. When you utilize ActiveX controls or components from the VB6 environment (such as the Winsock control or the ADO library), COM serves as the communication mechanism between your application and the external service. Although COM components were originally written in C++, Visual Basic 5 allowed developers to write their own COM components through its ActiveX DLL and ActiveX EXE project options.

Today there are literally thousands of ActiveX components that extend the functionality of Visual Basic in a variety ways. Components exist that offer advanced 3D graphing capability, disk compression, and message encryption. Because these components were authored before .NET, they are unmanaged as they execute outside the CLR. Naturally, many developers are concerned about their status in the .NET world.

Thankfully, Microsoft does not expect developers to abandon the large install base of ActiveX controls. Facilities exist to call both ActiveX controls and components from VB.NET. In Chapter 8, we examine COM Runtime Callable Wrappers (RCWs) that bridge the gap between the unmanaged world of ActiveX and the managed world of the CLR.

COM+

Windows 2000 introduced COM+, which is a collection of services that COM components can use to better their performance in the enterprise application setting. Some of these services include *transactions* (used when a component communicates with a database), *object pooling* (increases performance by reusing objects to avoid initialization overhead), and *queuing* (allows a client to asynchronously communicate with an object).

COM+ services can be used from the .NET Framework through the Base Class Libraries found in the `System.EnterpriseServices` namespace. The .NET Runtime also implicitly uses COM+ to support some of its services. Chapter 6 explains how the CLR automatically uses COM+ services behind the scenes to object pooling capability for managed classes.

SIMPLE EXAMPLE

In this example we will write the proverbial Hello World program in VB.NET. If you have not already done so, now would be a good time to consult Chapter 2 to ensure that you have properly installed the .NET Framework and VS.NET.

To illustrate the new capabilities of VB.NET, we will write three versions of the Hello World program:

1. A console application that we produce using the VB.NET command-line compiler (vbc.exe)

2. A console application that we create from the VS.NET IDE
3. A traditional "form" application that we also create from the VS.NET IDE

For those unfamiliar with the concept, a *console application* is a program that runs entirely within the command line (DOS prompt) with no graphical elements. The XCOPY.EXE utility that ships with all versions of Windows, for example, is a console application because its output is contained within the command prompt. Remember that VB.NET ships with a stand-alone compiler, allowing us to compile programs from the command prompt.

Hello World Application #1

Prior to VB.NET, Visual Basic development rarely proceeded outside the VB environment. In our first of many departures from the norm, we will not develop our application from an intuitive design environment, but will use a straightforward text editor. Bring up a text editor such as Notepad, and save the code in Listing 1.1 to a file called HelloWorld.vb.

```
'Reference the appropriate namespaces:
Imports System
Imports Microsoft.VisualBasic

Module HelloWorld
        Sub Main
                Console.WriteLine(UCase("Hello World!"))
        End Sub
End Module
```

Listing 1.1   Hello World console application

Listing 1.1 certainly does not look like VB code! Before we compile it from the command line, let's break it down line by line. First, note that we have used the UCase() function, which was an intrinsic function in VB6. In order to use this function, we must make use of the following rule:

Intrinsic VB elements like UCase and MsgBox are now accessed through the Microsoft.VisualBasic namespace.

As you may have surmised, this namespace contains elements that were previously a part of the VB Runtime: functions (UCase, isNothing), constants (vbNewLine, vbNullString), objects (Collection, Err), operators (And, Or, Not), and directives (#Const, #If, #EndIf).

Thus, to use `UCase`, we must reference the `Microsoft.VisualBasic` namespace as we did at the beginning of Listing 1.1. If you look above this line, you will see that we also referenced the `System` namespace. Among other things, the `System` namespace contains the types in the CTS (such as `Object`) and many of the basic .NET language features that we examine in Chapter 6. It is good practice to always reference the `System` namespace within programs. The `System` namespace also contains the `Console` class, which, as its name suggests, is a class that we can use for console operations such as outputting text to the command prompt.

Before we investigate the source in Listing 1.1 any further, we must examine yet another new feature of VB.NET: *shared members.*

Shared Members
In Visual Basic 6, before you could access the methods of a class, you had to instantiate the class:

```
dim s as new SomeClass   'instantiate the class
s.Foo()                  'call Foo
```

In VB.NET, you can write a class that exposes shared members. By designating a member as *shared,* it can be accessed without instantiating the class (if you are familiar with C++ or Java, you can think of *shared* as equivalent to *static*). Consider the class in Listing 1.2:

```
Class SomeClass

    Public Shared size as Integer
    Public Shared Sub MyMethod
        'Do something
    End Sub

    Public size2 as Integer
    Public Sub MyMethod2
        'Do something
    End Sub

End Class
```

Listing 1.2   Shared member declaration

As can be seen from Listing 1.2, `SomeClass` contains two methods (`MyMethod`, `MyMethod2`) and two member variables (`size` and `size2`). Because `size` and `MyMethod` are declared with the `Shared` keyword, they can be accessed without instantiating `SomeClass`:

```
SomeClass.size = 45    'Call shared members directly on
SomeClass.MyMethod     'SomeClass
```

If we wanted to access `size2` or `MyMethod2`, however, we would first have to create an instance of `SomeClass`:

```
dim s as new SomeClass
s.size2 = 45;
s.MyMethod2

'note that you can also call a static member on an instantiated
'class:
s.MyMethod
```

The term shared *member* may be confusing. In object-oriented terminology, a class's *methods* and *variables* are also called the class's *members*. Thus, in Listing 1.2, `MyMethod` is shared *method*, `size` is a shared *variable*, and both are also shared *members*.

Source Analysis Continued
The shared member concept is important because several classes in the Base Class Libraries contain shared members. One such example is the `Console` class that we use in Listing 1.1. This class exposes a shared method called `WriteLine()`, which outputs a string to the console.

Finally, note that in Listing 1.1 the call to `Console.WriteLine()` is enclosed within a method called `Main()`, which in turn is contained within a module called `HelloWorld`. Let us first consider the `Main()` method.

Remember that we are writing a console application. When we execute it from the command line, there must be some designated point at which the program begins its execution. This is in contrast to form-based applications developed in VB6, where you wrote code to respond to the user's actions (e.g., clicking a button).

If you are familiar with Java or C++, you are aware that a program's execution always begins with a method called `Main()`. So it is with VB.NET—console applications automatically start at the `Main()` method. If you try to write a console application without a `Main` method, VB.NET will politely display the following error message:

```
vbc : error BC30420: Startup 'Sub Main()' was not found in 'HelloWorld'
```

A console application's Main method must reside in a module. In Visual Basic 6, you added a module to a project when you wanted its contents (constants and methods) to be globally accessible throughout your application. The effect in VB.NET is similar—any members you place inside a VB.NET module are globally accessible throughout your application. Note that unlike VB6, modules do not have to be contained in separate files with a .bas extension. Instead, modules can reside directly in your application's code. This is also a good time to point out that VB.NET source files all end with the .vb extension, as opposed to a VB6 project that could contain .bas, .frm, .frx, and .vpb files.

Compiling and Running the Application
To compile the application in Listing 1.1, click on the VS.NET command prompt found in the VS.NET Tools folder (see Figure 1.1). (Again, consult Chapter 2 for installation details.)

Figure 1.1   The VS.NET command prompt

Save Listing 1.1 into a file called HelloWorld.vb, and execute the following line at the command prompt (make sure you are in the same directory where HelloWorld.vb is located):

```
vbc.exe HelloWorld.vb
```

You have just created your first VB.NET application! VBC.EXE will produce a file called HelloWorld.exe that displays "HELLO WORLD!" in the command prompt. It is important to realize that this executable will run only on a computer that has the .NET Framework installed. The applications produced by VB.NET are not the same as the ones created with VB6. Instead, they are a new type of component called an *assembly*. We examine assemblies in Chapter 5.

Recap
This example has illustrated some of the fundamental changes in VB.NET:

- VB.NET can create console applications, which are applications that contain no GUI elements. Console applications contain a mandatory `Main` method where program execution begins.
- VB.NET classes can contain shared members, which are class methods and variables that can be accessed without instantiating the class.
- VB.NET source files end with the `.vb` extension and can directly contain modules. All the members of a module are globally accessible from within the application.
- VB.NET includes its own command-line compiler that can produce applications outside the design environment.

In our next example, we will investigate the more familiar domain of an intuitive design environment—the VS.NET IDE.

Hello World Application #2

In this example we will re-create the application we wrote in Listing 1.1, but we will do it from the VS.NET IDE. Start Visual Studio.NET by going to the Microsoft Visual Studio.NET 7.0 folder in your Start menu. Invoke the VS.NET IDE by clicking the Microsoft Visual Studio.NET 7.0 icon. If you are running VS.NET for the first time, you will be asked to choose your preferred keyboard and window layout, as shown in Figure 1.2.

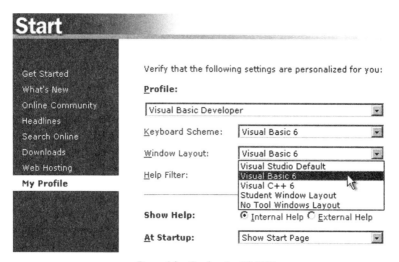

Figure 1.2   Configuring VS.NET

Remember that VS.NET now houses the development environments for VB.NET, Visual C++, and C#. Unless you want a different setup, choose the Visual Basic 6 profile, keyboard, and window schemes, as we have illustrated in Figure 1.2. Next, go to the File menu and select New → Project. This will bring up the dialog box in Figure 1.3.

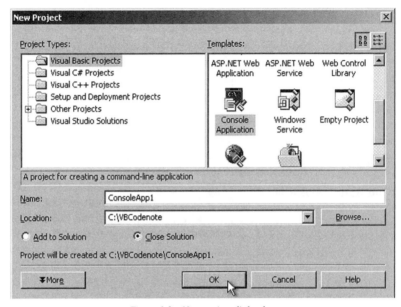

Figure 1.3   New project dialog box

As shown in Figure 1.3, choose Visual Basic Project under Project Type, and choose Console Application under Templates. Give your project a name and specify the directory where it will be stored. Click OK, and in a moment, VS.NET will create a Visual Basic console project for you. VS.NET automatically creates a file in your project called Module1.vb that contains the following code:

```
Module Module1

    Sub Main()

    End Sub

End Module
```

Because VS.NET knows that you are writing a console application, it automatically inserts a Main method into the source file (and encloses it within a module). Add the line Console.WriteLine(UCase("Hello

World")) to the Main method, and you now have a console application that is identical to the one we created in Listing 1.1. Unlike the previous example, however, we do not have to compile our application from the command line. Instead, you can compile and run your project directly from the VS.NET environment by going to the Debug menu and clicking Start (or you could simply press F5).

You may have noticed that we did not reference the Microsoft.VisualBasic and System namespaces as we did in Listing 1.1. VS.NET saves us some extra typing by automatically referencing these namespaces for us (as well as additional, commonly used namespaces that we will examine in other chapters).

The VS.NET IDE may seem foreign to some developers, as it looks nothing like the VB6 design environment. This is because we are creating a console application. In the next example we will create a form-based application, where the VS.NET IDE will take on a more familiar face.

Hello World Application #3
In this example we will create a third version of the Hello World application. Unlike the previous two examples, this application will be the familiar form type that Visual Basic developers have always designed. Close the console project we created in the previous example, go to File menu, and select New → Project. You will once again be greeted with the dialog box shown in Figure 1.3. This time, select Window Application under the project template and click OK. Wait a moment, and VS.NET will manifest itself into the more familiar design environment depicted in Figure 1.4.

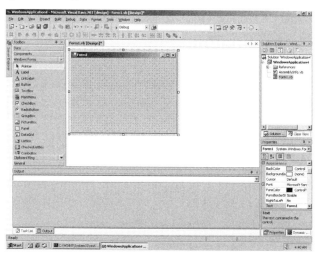

Figure 1.4   VS.NET design environment

Take a minute to explore the VS.NET IDE, and you will see several recognizable elements from VB6: the toolbox, which contains controls such as buttons and textboxes, the Property Inspector, the Project Explorer (now called the Solution Explorer) and of course, the form design window.

Drag a button onto the form, double-click it, and insert the following highlighted code into the button's click event:

```
Private Sub Button1_Click(ByVal sender As System.Object, ByVal e As
System.EventArgs) Handles Button1.Click
        MessageBox.Show("Hello World")
End Sub
```

Listing 1.3   Hello World program using MessageBox

Note that in the Listing 1.3 we used `MessageBox.Show()` to display a message box. Although we could have used `MsgBox` (it is included in the `Microsoft.VisualBasic` namespace for backward compatibility), the proper way to design desktop applications in the .NET Framework is to use the new Windows Forms classes, such as `MessageBox`. The benefits of doing so are twofold:

1. Windows Forms classes provide capabilities not found in previous versions of VB (as illustrated in Chapter 7).
2. Understanding the Windows Forms classes is essential when interoperating with other languages in the .NET Framework. Developers writing .NET applications in other languages (e.g., C#) may not be aware of VB-intrinsic functions like `MsgBox`, and they are likely to use the Windows Forms classes.

Also note from Listing 1.3 that the button's click event is considerably more complex than its VB6 equivalent (note the two additional arguments and the `Handles` keyword). Understanding VB.NET's new event structure requires concepts examined in Chapter 6. For now, just proceed with the knowledge that, as in Visual Basic 6, the button's click event will get called whenever the button is clicked. Run the application by pressing F5, click the form's button, and a "Hello World" message box will appear on the screen.

SORTING EXAMPLE

To round out this chapter, we present an example a little more pragmatic
than the perfunctory Hello World application—sorting an array of numbers. C and C++ programmers have traditionally relied on the C runtime
library for such functionality. The universality of the Base Class Libraries means that Visual Basic programmers can also enjoy the luxury
of prewritten routines. The VB.NET example in Listing 1.4 uses the
BCL's ArrayList class to sort through a list of 10 random numbers.

```vbnet
'Use the System and System.Collections namespaces
Imports System
Imports System.Collections

Module SortingExample
Sub Main()
   dim k as integer
   dim oArray as ArrayList
   dim oRandom as Random

   oArray = new ArrayList()
   oRandom = new Random()

   'Add ten random numbers to the list:
   for k = 0 to 9
      oArray.Add(oRandom.Next() mod 100) 'add random #'s 0-99
   next

   oArray.Sort()   'That's it!

   'Print out the sorted numbers:
   for k= 0 to 9
      Console.Write(oArray(k))
      Console.Write(",")
    next
End Sub
end module
```

Listing 1.4   Using the Base Class Libraries to sort numbers

Save Listing 1.4 into a file called SortNumbers.vb, and compile it
using the following command line (alternatively you could create a console project in VS.NET):

```
vbc.exe SortNumbers.vb
```

The SortNumbers.exe application that is created produces output similar to the following:

```
10,11,61,63,74,77,80,90,94,98,
```

The bolded portions of Listing 1.4 illustrate areas where the Base Class Libraries are being utilized and are worth more explanation.

```
Imports System
Imports System.Collections
```

The two preceding lines inform VB.NET that we will be using the System and System.Collection namespaces. Remember that namespaces are a syntactical shortcut that saves us from having to fully qualify the BCL classes when we reference them. The following two lines instantiate the BCL classes that we will use:

```
oArray = new ArrayList() 'no Set !
oRandom = new Random()
```

The ArrayList class is like a collection; elements can be added and removed and it will automatically resize itself. The Random class generates the random numbers that we will sort. Note that the VB.NET syntax does *not* require the Set keyword when instantiating classes (a change we revisit in Chapter 3).

```
for k = 0 to 9
    oArray.Add(oRandom.Next() mod 100)
next

oArray.Sort()   'That's it!
```

The preceding code fragment adds 10 random numbers to the list and sorts the array. This simply involves calling the Sort() method against the ArrayList class—the underlying operation is handled by the BCL class.

As can be seen from the code in Listing 1.4, using the BCL is simply a matter of understanding the conventions of the classes you are calling. In the preceding example, the functionality of the program (sorting and output) is provided by the BCL; VB.NET simply acts as a forum to call it. To a large degree, using VB.NET to develop .NET applications is a matter of syntactical preference due to the universality of the Base Class Libraries. For example, we could have written a C# program identical to the one in Listing 1.4 that used `ArrayList` to sort 10 numbers. The language neutrality of the CLR means that your knowledge of the Base Class Libraries is immediately transferable to other .NET languages.

Some of you may be wondering why we did not use Visual Basic's `Rnd` function to generate random numbers. Again, although we could have done this (`Rnd` is also found in the `Microsoft.VisualBasic` namespace), the general practice under the .NET Framework is to use the newer BCL equivalents where possible.

HOW AND WHY

Where Do the Base Class Libraries Reside?
In our examples thus far, we have used BCL classes/functions such as `UCase` and `ArrayList` by appropriately referencing the namespaces in which they are contained. Where, however, do these classes actually reside (i.e., which files contain their implementation code)?

As of this writing, the BCL classes can be found in the following directory (where `versionNum` is the particular version of the .NET Framework you have installed):

`\%winroot%\Microsoft.NET\Framework\versionNum\`

If you look in this directory, you will find several DLLs that contain the BCL classes for a given namespace (some DLLs actually contain numerous namespaces). Table 1.1 lists some of the more important files in the .NET Framework.

DLL	Contents
`Mscorlib.dll`	Core classes in the System namespace
`Microsoft.VisualBasic.dll`	Classes/functions for VB6 backwards compatibility
`System.Data.dll`	ADO.NET classes—the new data access mechanism
`Systen.Drawing.dll`	GDI+ classes; a powerful graphics package.
`System.EnterpriseServices.dll`	Classes to access COM+ services
`System.WindowsForms.dll`	Windows Forms classes

Table 1.1   Important DLLs containing BCL classes

The Base Class Library DLLs are packaged as assemblies. In Chapter 5, we will see how you can inspect an assembly to determine all the classes it contains.

It should now be clear why the .NET Framework must be installed on a computer in order to execute VB.NET applications. When we use a BCL class or function like UCase, the CLR determines the DLL in which the function is located and loads it appropriately when the application is executed.

Can I Call Functions in the Microsoft.VisualBasic Namespace from Other .NET Languages Like C# or Managed C++?
From the previous question, you can see that the Microsoft .VisualBasic.dll file contains classes and functions for VB6 backward capability. In Chapter 5, we see that the Base Class Library files are packaged assemblies that contain language-independent IL code. Therefore, any .NET compiler will be able to access any BCL class.

This means that the functions in the Microsoft.VisualBasic namespace can also be called by managed C++ and C# developers (try convincing a C++ programmer to use MsgBox, however). As we have cautioned, the general rule of thumb is to shy away from using intrinsic VB functions such as MsgBox and to use their newer BCL equivalents.

Chapter Summary

VB.NET significantly revamps the Visual Basic language in a number of areas. Various elements of the language syntax, such as arrays, control properties, and classes, have fundamentally changed. Other entities, such as the Variant data type, have been removed all together. VB.NET also introduces several new concepts into the Visual Basic domain, such as object inheritance, multithreading, and shared class members.

Many of these changes are by-products of VB.NET's new home—the .NET Framework, which fundamentally alters the way applications run under the Windows operating system. Under .NET, applications execute under the auspices of the Common Language Runtime (CLR), which can be thought of as an evolved version of the Visual Basic Runtime. Like the VB Runtime, the CLR provides services such as automatic memory management, type safety-checking, and exception handling. Unlike the VB Runtime, the CLR is not exclusively linked to programs written in VB. Any language that can be compiled to Microsoft Intermediate Language (IL) code can execute within the CLR. In addition to VB.NET, Microsoft's next version of Visual Studio (VS.NET) contains

IL compilers for C# and managed C++. Code that executes inside the CLR is called *managed code*. Code running outside the CLR (like code produced by previous versions of VB and Visual C++) is said to be *unmanaged code*.

The CLR also supersedes the functionality of the Visual Basic Runtime in a number of ways. As we show in Chapter 5, for example, the CLR's ability to interpret intrinsically neutral IL code allows applications written in different languages to seamlessly interoperate. Another feature of the CLR is garbage collection which, as we see in Chapter 6, has interesting repercussions for the manner in which objects must release their resources.

The second important entity in the .NET Framework is the Base Class Libraries (BCL), which serve as the building blocks for VB.NET applications. The BCL houses functions that were previously native functions of the Visual Basic language (e.g., InStr and UCase). The BCL also contains hundreds of classes for such tasks as remote messaging, File IO, and data access. Because the BCL classes are packaged as language-neutral IL code, they can be accessed from other .NET languages in addition to VB.NET. The Base Class Libraries are organized in hierarchical manner using namespaces, which are syntactical shortcuts that make calling classes easier.

In addition to syntax changes, the Visual Basic IDE is now a thing of the past. VS.NET now houses the development environments for VB.NET, C++, and C#. VB.NET also includes a command-line compiler that allows you to produce applications outside the design environment.

Chapter 2

—

INSTALLATION

As of this writing the .NET Framework is still in beta. Thus, the contents of this chapter are subject to change. Please consult the online reference at ⊶VB020001 for up-to-date installation instructions.

SYSTEM REQUIREMENTS

In order to install the .NET Framework on your machine, Microsoft recommends the following system configuration:

- **Processor**   Minimum, Pentium II-450 MHz (Pentium III 650 MHz recommended)
- **Operating system**   Windows 2000 (Server or Professional), Windows XP, or Windows NT 4.0 Server.
- **Memory**   Windows 2000 Professional: 96 MB (128 MB recommended), Windows 2000 Server: 192 MB (256 MB recommended)
- **Hard drive**   500 MB free on the drive where the OS is installed (usually C:\), and 2.5 gigs free on the installation drive (where VS.NET will be installed)

.NET DISTRIBUTION

VS.NET and the .NET Framework is distributed on four CDs. The first three contain the VS.NET development tools, and the fourth contains the Windows Component Update. The Windows Component Update will install the core framework files (the CLR, Runtime classes) and updated versions of system files that the Framework requires in order to run on your machine. For information on obtaining the CDs either by mail or download, please see /www.microsoft.com/net/.

INSTALLING .NET

To install the .NET Framework, run SETUP.EXE found on the first CD. After a couple of minutes, you will be greeted with the screen in Figure 2.1.

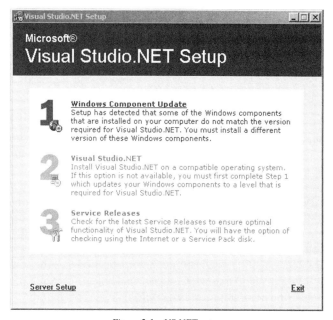

Figure 2.1   VS.NET setup

As Figure 2.1 indicates, you must run the Windows Component Update before installing VS.NET. After clicking Windows Component Update, the setup program will analyze your machine for a few minutes to determine which system files need to be updated. Depending on the operating system and the application that you have already installed, the setup program may have to reboot the system several times during the installation process. Because of this, it offers the Automatic Log On feature depicted in Figure 2.2.

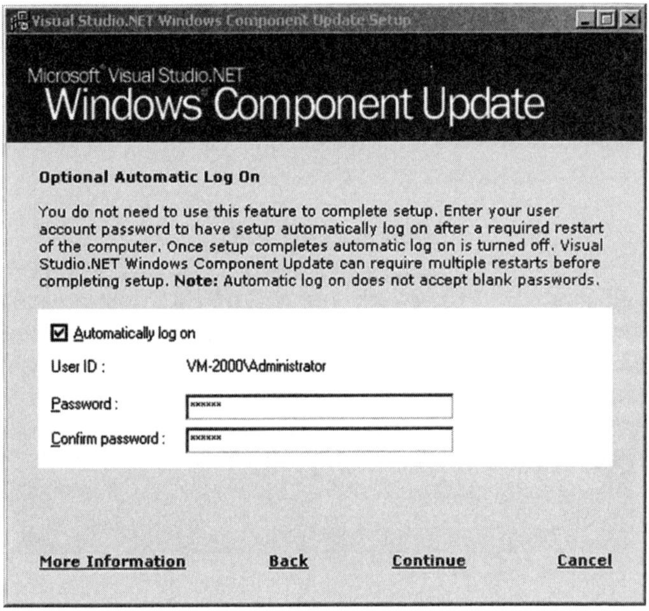

Figure 2.2   Automatic log on

By supplying your password as shown in Figure 2.2, the system can automatically log on and continue the installation every time it has to reboot the machine. Because the setup program may have to reboot the machine as many as seven times during the installation routine, this option can be a real time-saver. If you disable this option, you will have to log onto the machine each time the computer reboots. (As of this writing, there are some beta issues with automatic log on, so please consult VB020002 for the latest information.)

After either enabling or disabling Automatic Log On, the setup program will begin the Windows Component Update. Depending on the files it must update, this procedure could take several minutes. During this time the setup program will detail its progress, as illustrated in Figure 2.3.

After the Windows Component Update has completed, the setup program will prompt you for the first VS.NET CD. It will then ask you to choose which portions of VS.NET you want installed (the IDE, MSDN documentation, etc.). The options screen is shown in Figure 2.4.

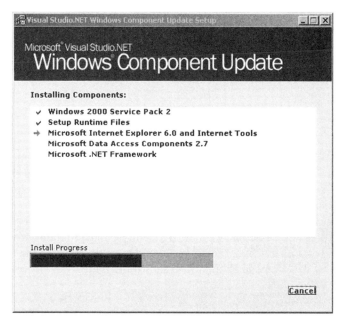

Figure 2.3   Windows Component Update in progress

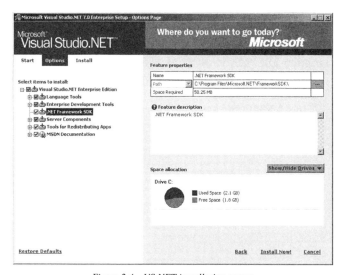

Figure 2.4   VS.NET installation screen

After selecting those aspects of VS.NET that you want included (VB.NET is contained under Language Tools in Figure 2.4), click Install Now. (For the purposes of working with the examples in this book, we recommend that you accept the default install options.) The setup program will begin. Depending on the options you have selected, installation could take anywhere from 20 to 60 minutes. After the installation has completed, your computer will contain all of the necessary tools to build and deploy .NET applications.

PROGRAM LOCATIONS

The .NET setup program will append two new items to your Start menu's Program folder. The first item is called Microsoft .NET Framework SDK and contains MSDN documentation and code samples. The second item is called Microsoft Visual Studio.NET 7.0 and contains links to the VS.NET IDE and to another folder called Visual Studio. NET Tools. In this book we will frequently build programs from the VS.NET command line, which you can access by clicking the Visual Studio.NET Command Prompt icon shown in Figure 2.5.

Figure 2.5   The Visual Studio.NET Command Prompt

Note that many utilities we use throughout *Codenotes for VB.NET* (e.g., ILDASM.EXE and SN.EXE, both in Chapter 5) are found in the \%Program Files%\Microsoft.NET\FrameworkSDK\Bin directory. If you use the VS.NET Command Prompt shown in Figure 2.5, this directory will automatically be included in your Path variable, so that you can access the .NET Framework utilities from within any directory.

Chapter 3

—

VB.NET SYNTAX CHANGES

This chapter examines many of the significant syntax changes from Visual Basic 6 to VB.NET. Given the many changes we will highlight in this chapter, one might claim that VB.NET is not really Visual Basic, but a slightly recognizable cousin. Indeed, many fundamental elements of the language, such as the Variant data type, are no longer supported by the new version of VB. In addition to syntactical changes, VB.NET also alters the language's scoping rules, the behavior of default properties, and the passing of procedure parameters. The language now includes powerful exception handling constructs, syntactical shortcuts for common arithmetic operations, and new variable declaration capabilities.

Although it is easy to become alarmed with the magnitude of changes in this new incarnation of VB, keep in mind that many of the syntax elements abolished by VB.NET resulted in confusing code listings that were difficult to debug. While transitioning to VB.NET can initially be frustrating, the language is now considerably cleaner than its predecessors. It is fair to say that many of the design decisions in VB.NET were done in the interest of the long-term evolution of the product, as opposed to short-term compatibility concerns.

At the end of this chapter we will examine VB.NET's Upgrade Wizard, which converts VB6 code to VB.NET. Even with the Upgrade Wizard, however, moving a VB6 project to the .NET framework is not a seamless process. Since many VB6 syntax elements and controls have no equivalent in VB.NET, you must manually overhaul these sections of your program by writing functionally similar VB.NET code.

Topic: Data Types

Developers are well acquainted with the intrinsic data types in VB6, such as Strings, Integers, and Variants. One of the challenges of VB.NET was to integrate native VB6 types with the common type system imposed by the CLR. In this topic, we examine the consequences of this integration.

CONCEPTS

The Object Type

One of the most significant changes in VB.NET is the removal of the Variant data type. As explained in Chapter 1, the Variant has been replaced with the System.Object type.

From a functional point of view, the Variant and System.Object types are equivalent. Both can store any of the permissible data types of their respective environments. Just as you used the Variant to store strings, integers, and classes in VB6, you can use System.Object to do the same in VB.NET:

```
Dim o As Object
o = "Hello World"
o = 33
o = someClass 'A reference to some class we have
```

Listing 3.1   System.Object in VB.NET

As can be seen from Listing 3.1, an Object is very much like a Variant. In fact, if you try to create a Variant variable in VS.NET, the IDE will automatically convert it into an Object (try this in the IDE). Although this change may seem nothing more than the renaming of syntax, an Object is more than just a Variant-like data type. You can do everything with an Object that you can with a Variant, but you can also do a lot more.

The Class Object

In addition to being able to hold any data type in VB.NET, an Object is also a class that exposes methods. Some of these methods (such as one called Finalize()) are used for .NET system services and will be examined in later chapters. Other ones, such as GetType(), can be used for informational purposes. For example, if you wanted to determine the underlying data type that an Object is holding you can use the following code:

```
Module Module1
    Sub Main()
        Dim o As Object

        o = "Hello World"
        Console.WriteLine("{0} is a {1}", o, o.GetType.FullName())
        o = 33
        Console.WriteLine("{0} is a {1}", o, o.GetType.FullName())
    End Sub
End Module
```

Listing 3.2   Using Object's GetType.FullName() method

If you copy Listing 3.2 into a Console project in VS.NET and run it, you will see the following output:

```
Hello World is a System.String
33 is a System.Int32
```

Remember from our first Hello World example in Chapter 1 that VB.NET console applications begin their execution at a `Main()` method and must be enclosed within a module. As with that example, we have employed the `Console.WriteLine()` method to output information to the screen. The `WriteLine()` syntax in Listing 3.2 might be new to some developers. Placing `{0}` and `{1}` in `WriteLine()`'s output string instructs the `Console` class to replace these tokens with the arguments that follow. In the first output line, `{0}` is replaced with whatever the variable `o` is holding, in this case "Hello World." Similarly, `{1}` is replaced with the second argument, which resolves to `System.String`. Throughout these CodeNotes we will use this method to output information. If you are familiar with C or C++, you will find this syntax similar to the `%` operator in the `printf` function.

As Listing 3.2 demonstrates, we can use an Object's `GetType` `.FullName()` method to determine the data type it is housing (you can still use VB6 operators such as `isNumeric`, `isDate`, etc.). A full listing of `Object`'s methods can be found at ⌖VB030001. We will revisit some of them in Chapter 6, when we look at garbage collection (which uses `Finalize()`) and reflection (which uses `GetType()`).

Everything Is an Object

You will frequently hear that every data type in VB.NET *is* an `Object`. This statement requires careful qualification. As previously outlined, there are two properties of the `Object` type in VB.NET:

1. An Object can house any data type in VB.NET (integers, strings, etc.).
2. An Object is a class that exposes methods such as GetType() and ToString().

To say that every data type is an Object is to say that it exposes all the methods of Object (the second point). Thus, integers and strings expose methods such as GetType and Finalize():

```
Dim I As Integer
Console.WriteLine("I is a {0}", I.GetType.FullName())


'the preceding code prints out:
I is a System.Int32
```

Listing 3.3   Everything is an Object

As Listing 3.3 illustrates, you can use the GetType.FullName() method on an Integer. We will explain why an Integer claims that it's a System.Int32 in the upcoming section on value types. If an Integer were truly an Object, however, it would adhere to the first property we have listed—it could store any VB.NET data type. We know that this is not the case for Integer objects (they cannot store strings, for example).

So, realize the claim that every data type is an Object is only partially true. (When we cover class derivation in Chapter 4, we will see this statement is most accurately rephrased as follows: Every data type in VB.NET *derives* from an Object.)

Reference Type and Value Types

In VB.NET a data type can be either a reference type or a value type. To understand the difference between the two, consider when you use the New keyword in VB6:

```
Dim a As Integer       'no New()
Dim b As New someClass 'New()
```

Listing 3.4   Reference and value type in VB6

In VB6, literal elements such as Integers and Strings are not declared using the New keyword. When instantiating a class, however, the New keyword is used (either when the variable is declared or when using the Set keyword thereafter).

In VB.NET, a value type is one that is declared without a New statement. Such types include all numeric data types, booleans, dates, structures (Types), and enumerations. As with VB6, reference types such as classes must be declared using New. In VB.NET, however, you no longer use the Set keyword to instantiate such a class:

```
Dim b As someClass
b = New someClass  'No Set keyword in VB.ENT
```

The primary difference between reference and value types lies in how the CLR allocates memory for each type. When you use a value type such as an integer, it is stored in an area called the *stack*—a fixed amount of memory that the CLR gives each VB.NET application. When you instantiate a reference type, it is stored in an entity called the *heap*—a block of memory that can dynamically change its size depending on your application's requirements.

The upshot of these different memory storehouses is that reference and value types are treated differently by the CLR. For example, reference types are garbage-collected whereas value types are not. In practice, VB.NET hides these differences from you. One area of interest, however, is how you test a reference type for equality.

Comparing Reference Types
As in VB6, if you wish to compare to reference types for equality you must use the is operator (not =, which you use for value types):

```
Dim a As New SomeClass
Dim b As New SomeClass

If a Is b Then
    Console.WriteLine("They are equal")
End If
```

Listing 3.5 Comparing reference types in VB.NET

Remember, reference types are considered equal if they are the same *instance* of a type. Because a and b are different instances of SomeClass, nothing will be printed. If we wanted to test whether a and b were of the same type, we would use System.Object.GetType() method as follows:

```
Dim a As New SomeClass()
Dim b As New SomeClass()

If a.GetType Is b.GetType Then
    Console.WriteLine("They are equal")
End If
```

Listing 3.6 Comparing for type equality in VB.NET

Exceptions to the Rule

The rules we have given for value and reference types would be simple and succinct were it not for two exceptions: strings and arrays. Although both these elements are reference types (they are allocated on the heap and garbage-collected), they adhere to value type semantics. This means the following for both strings and arrays:

1. They are not dimensioned with the New keyword.
2. They are tested for equality using the = operator.

These semantics are identical to the syntax you used in VB6. You may wonder why the CLR stores strings and arrays on the heap and not in the stack. Recall that the heap is an area of memory whose size can change dynamically (whereas a stack's cannot). Since the size of both strings and arrays can change (an array's length can grow or shrink using the ReDim keyword), it makes sense to store these types on the heap.

VB.NET Value Types

The CTS and VB.NET

The Common Type System (CTS) is the basis for all types in VB.NET. In addition to defining the System.Object type we previously examined, the CTS also defines commonly used types such as integers (System.Int32), booleans (System.Boolean), and doubles (System.Double). When you use the Integer data type in your applications, VB.NET converts it to a System.Int32 behind the scenes (refer to Listing 3.3). Table 3.1 shows how CTS data types map to the intrinsic ones in VB.NET.

VB6 type	VB.NET equivalent type	underlying CTS type
Byte (1)	Byte (1)	System.Byte
Boolean (2)	Boolean (4)	System.Boolean
Currency (8)	Decimal (12)	System.Decimal
Single (4)	Single (4)	System.Single
Double (8)	Double (8)	System.Double
Integer (2)	Short (4)	System.Int16
Long (4)	Integer (4)	System.Int32
N/A	Long (8)	System.Int64

Table 3.1   CTS data types used in VB.NET (brackets indicate size in bytes)

As Table 3.1 illustrates, V6's Currency data type has been supplanted with the more capable Decimal type. VB.NET also includes the new Char type (not shown in Table 3.1), which can be used when you want to call Windows API functions that accept strings (see ∘ᴺ⥿VB030002 for details).

User-Defined Types
In VB6, you used the Type keyword to create your own custom types:

```
Public Type Player
      Name As String
      Position As String
End Type
```

In VB.NET, you instead use the Structure keyword (also note the presence of the Dim keyword):

```
Public Structure Player
      Dim Name As String
      Dim Position As String
End Structure
```

VB.NET Reference Types

Strings
Even though a String adheres to value type semantics, it is really a reference type. When you use the String data type in VB.NET, it utilizes the System.String class behind the scenes. Although you can still use VB6 string operators such as Mid() and Left(), you can frequently use the members of System.String to accomplish the same thing:

```
Dim s As String
s = "Hello World"


'Both Lines print out Hello:
Console.WriteLine(s.Substring(0, 4)) 'substring() starts at 0!
Console.WriteLine(Mid(s, 1, 5))      'Mid starts at 1
```

Listing 3.7   The System.String class

As Listing 3.7 illustrates, you can use either the Mid() or System.String.SubString() method to extract "Hello" from "Hello World." In addition to methods of System.String, you will also find string helper classes in the System.Text and System.IO namespaces. For details see ♦^{CN}VB030003.

Fixed-Length Strings

VB.NET does not allow fixed-length strings. If you want a string of finite length you must use VB.NET's new Char data type. You normally use fixed-length strings in VB.NET when interfacing with the Windows API.

```
dim s as string * 100    'Not valid in VB.NET!
dim s(100) as Char       'Use char instead
```

Array Bounds

All arrays in VB.NET are zero-based; you cannot dimension an array using the To construct. In addition, you can no longer use VB6's Option Base command to set the first index value.

```
dim a(5 To 10)           'not valid in VB.NET
dim a(10)                'VB.NET creates elements 0 to 10.
```

Option Strict

VB.NET includes a new specifier called Option Strict that restricts the implicit type conversions it can perform. For example, the following code compiles under both VB6 and VB.NET:

```
Dim A As Integer
Dim B As Long
A = B            'dangerous, because B can store larger #'s than A
```

The problem with the preceding assignment is that the Long variable (B) *may* contain too large a value for the Integer to store. If the value of B happens to be too large for A to handle, both languages will generate overflow exceptions.

By placing Option Strict On at the top of your source file, you are telling VB.NET not to implicitly cast variables that may be too large for their holders (what is called *narrowing conversion*). As a result, VB.NET will not compile the preceding code. To perform the assignment, you must explicitly inform VB.NET that you are aware of the dangers by using the CInt() function:

```
Option Strict On
...
Dim A As Integer
```

```
Dim B As Long
A = CInt(B)
```

Although VB.NET will compile the preceding code, an overflow exception will *still* occur if the value of B is too large for an Integer. By explicitly casting using CInt(), you are simply avoiding the compiler error. It is your responsibility to handle any errors that result from a problematic assignment.

Keep in mind that the reverse assignment (b = a) will always compile. This is because a Long can store anything represented by an Integer. The assignment of a variable with smaller storage requirements than its holder is called a *widening conversion*. Widening conversions are always permissible under VB.NET, irrespective of Option Strict.

New Declaration Capabilities

VB.NET includes a host of new variable declaration facilities. These are illustrated in the following code block:

```
'in VB6, only "a" would be a Long (the rest would be variants)
'in VB.NET, all four variables are now Longs:
dim a,b,c,d as Long

'In VB.NET you can now initialize in the declaration line:
dim e as Integer = 6


'VB.NET permits multiple type declarations on the same line:
dim f as Integer, g as string


'You can now initialize an array in the declaration line:
dim h() as Integer = {3,4,5}
```

Listing 3.8   New declaration capabilities in VB.NET

Collections

VB.NET supports two types of collections. The first, is a VB6-style collection exposed by the Microsoft.VisualBasic.Collection class. As in VB6, this collection is a generic container (it holds System.Objects instead of Variants).

Newer collection classes can be found in the System.Collections namespace. If you look in this namespace you will find classes that offer different collection properties. The StringCollection class, for example, stores a series of strings. The Queue class simulates the behavior of a queue data structure (elements must be removed in order from first to last in the collection). A more detailed description of the classes in System.Collections can be found at ⊶VB030004.

Note that a VB6-style Collection and those found in System.Collections are *not* interchangeable; a method that expects one type of collection will not accept a collection of the second type. If you are exposing methods that will be used by C# or managed C++ developers, you will probably want to use the newer, more capable classes in System.Collections. VB6-style collections should be used solely in VB.NET.

SUMMARY

In addition to replacing the Variant data type with System.Object, VB.NET changes the properties of strings, arrays, and object instantiation. All arrays are now zero-based, rendering the Option Base and To keywords obsolete. To manipulate strings, you can now use the methods in the System.String class in addition to VB6 functions such as Mid() and IntStr(). Custom types are now defined using the Structure keyword as opposed to Type, and you no longer use Set when instantiating objects.

VB.NET also introduces some new data type features into the language. The Option Strict On directive informs VB.NET not to perform hazardous type conversions implicitly. New data types, such as the decimal and long integers (64 bits) are now native members of the language. Finally, VB.NET includes a host of new variable declaration features, such as the ability to initialization variables when they are declared.

Topic: VB.NET Exception Handling

One of the more primitive aspects of Visual Basic has always been its error handling mechanisms. With the introduction of exception handling, VB.NET can now cope with errors as smoothly as Java or C++. To appreciate the sophistication of exception handling, consider how you handled errors in Visual Basic 6 using the straightforward On Error Goto statement:

```
Private Function Div(num As Long, den As Long) As Long

    On Error GoTo DivByZero
```

```
    Divide = num / den
    Exit Function

DivByZero:
    Debug.Print "Divide by Zero Error"
End Function
```

Listing 3.9   VB6's On Error Goto

The primary limitation with On Error Goto is that it allows only one active error handler per function. What this means is that if we added a second On Error Goto to Listing 3.9, it would supplant the first one (errors would be directed to the new error handler). Multiple errors handlers in the same function cannot, therefore, be nested—if one routine cannot manage a given error, the error cannot propagate a second, more capable routine.

Another problem with this stipulation is that if we wish to catch errors in an error handler itself, we must use another On Error Goto. This recursive technique often results in ungainly code that is difficult to follow. VB.NET's introduction of structured exception handling strengthens the language's error handling capabilities considerably.

CONCEPTS

Structured Exception Handling

Structured error handling involves three new VB.NET keywords: Try, Catch, and Finally. With structured error handling, you break up code into execution blocks, each of which has its own error handler. Let us first consider how Try, Catch, and Finally work:

```
Private Function Divide(ByVal num As Integer, ByVal den As Integer)
As Integer

    Dim answer As Integer
    Try
        answer = num \ den
    Catch
        denominator = 1
        Answer = num \ den
    Finally
        Divide = Answer
```

```
    End Try

End Function
```

Listing 3.10   Structured error handling in VB.NET

Any code that might raise an error is placed after the `Try` keyword. If this code executes without fail, then the code in the `Catch` section is skipped and the code in the `Finally` block is executed. If the code generates an error, however, control is transferred to the `Catch` block where the error can be remedied (notice the `Catch` block in Listing 3.10 rectifies the situation where a denominator might be zero).

A notable property of structured exception handling is that a `Finally` block will *always* execute after the code in a `Try` block. Thus, even if the code in a `Try` block does something abrupt (performs a `GoTo` or `Exit Function`), the code in `Finally` will execute before the jump is performed. The `Finally` block is normally used to perform cleanup code such as closing file handles and database connections. Note that `Finally` is an optional keyword in the `try/catch` structure—use it only if you have code that must run before exiting the exception block.

Nested Exceptions

You may be wondering what happens if either a `Catch` or `Finally` block raises an error. Consider a related question in VB6: What occurs if a function's own error handler generates an error—what if the code after `DivByZero` in Listing 3.9 does something illegal? In this case, the error propagates to whomever called `Divide()`. If the calling routine doesn't have an error handler, the error propagates to its caller and so on. If subsequent callers cannot handle the error, the error will eventually propagate to the VB Runtime, which will shut down the application. Similarly, if the `Finally` block in Listing 3.10 does something illegal, its caller will receive the error and so forth. VB.NET's last line of defense is not the VB Runtime, of course, but the CLR.

Although the propagation behavior just described is an adequate defense against problematic error handlers, structured exception handling offers a more elegant solution. You can enclose one `Try` block within another, a technique often referred to as *nested exceptions*. Nested exceptions allow you to localize your "error-error" handling code:

```
Try
     'A second try block:
     Try
          'Some code
     Catch
```

```
        'Rectification code
    Finally
            a = 1 /0  'divide by zero!
    End Try


Catch
    'The error is caught here
Finally


End Try
```

Listing 3.11   Nested exceptions

Now if the inner `Catch` or `Finally` blocks do something illegal, the error will be caught by the outer `Catch` block.

Listing 3.3 may seem like a contrived example. After all, what are the chances that our own error handling code will result in an error? Nonetheless, a good developer always plans for the boundary cases. Not surprisingly, nested exceptions have other uses. We can prescribe, for example, that an inner `Try` block handle only certain types of errors, while the outer `Try` block handles the rest. In order to use nested exceptions in this fashion, we must understand how errors are represented in the .NET Framework using exception classes.

Exceptions Classes

In Visual Basic 6 you used the `Err` object to determine the type of error that was generated. It is not uncommon for error handlers to use this object to deal appropriately with different types of errors:

```
On Error GoTo ErrorRoutine
        'IO Operations...


ErrorRoutine:
Select Case Err.Number
    Case 11 'Division by zero
        'Rectify division problem
    Case 53 File not found
        'Rectify file problem
    Case Else 'All other errors
        '...
End Select
```

Listing 3.12   The Err object

Although you can still use the Err object in VB.NET (it is found in the Microsoft.VisualBasic namespace), the representation of errors in the .NET Framework has evolved into exception classes. Under this model, error information is communicated through unique classes in the BCL. A divide-by-zero error, for example, is represented through the DivideByZeroException class. Similarly, a file-not-found error is signified through the FileNotFoundException class.

Like all BCL classes, exception classes are located in an appropriate namespace. FileNotFoundException, for example, is found in System.IO, and HttpException is found in System.Web. You use exception classes in the following manner:

```
Try
        'Normal code over here.
Catch divError As DivideByZeroException
        MsgBox divError.Message
Catch fileError As FileNotFoundException
        MsgBox fileError.FileName
Catch
        'All other errors
End Try
```

Listing 3.13   Exception classes

As Listing 3.13 illustrates, you can have multiple Catch statements in one Try block, each of which handles a different type of error. If the code in Listing 3.13 generates a division-by-zero error, control is transferred to the first Catch block. Once inside this block, we can scrutinize the divError object for information. In Listing 3.13, we just print out error information using the class's Message property.

Notice, that in Listing 3.13 each Catch block is dealing with a different exception class (excluding the last Catch block, which we will get to momentarily). So, whereas divError is a DivideByZeroException, fileError is a FileNotFoundException. Not surprisingly, fileError has methods that divError does not. In Listing 3.13, for example, we print out the name of the problematic file using the fileError.FileName() method. A file name does not make sense in the context of a division error, so DivideByZeroException does not expose a FileName() method.

The second point is that the object names (divError and fileError) used within a given Catch block are arbitrary; you determine what they are called. You will commonly see try/catch blocks where the exception objects are more succinctly and consistently named:

```
Catch e As DivideByZeroException
      MsgBox e.Message
Catch e As FileNotFoundException
      MsgBox e.FileName
```

Listing 3.14   Exception class convention

The last Catch block in Listing 3.13 catches any errors not handled in the first two blocks. The downside of a block declared in such a manner (a Catch construct by itself) is that there is no exception object that you can query for error information. The way around this shortcoming is to replace the last Catch line with something like this:

```
Catch unknownError As Exception
```

This line catches any type of error and stores associated information in a generic Exception class. As explained in the inheritance topic in Chapter 4, because all exception classes *derive* from the Exception class, the preceding line will catch *all* exceptions (assuming the exception hasn't been caught by a previous Catch block). This raises an important point: The order of your Catch blocks matters! If we made the preceding Catch block the first block in Listing 3.13, all exceptions would be caught by this block instead of traveling down to a more specific and appropriate exception class (such as DivideByZeroException if the exception is a division by zero). In other words, you should always list your Catch blocks in order from most specific to least specific.

You can also define your own types of exceptions by writing custom exception classes. For details see ⌖VB030005.

The When Keyword

The Catch construct can also be used with a keyword called When, which allows you to use a logical expression to determine if a given block will catch errors:

```
Catch e As DivideByZeroException When someVar = 1
      MsgBox e.Message
```

If there is a division-by-zero error, the preceding code will only catch it if someVar is 1. Otherwise, the error will propagate to the following Catch blocks (if there are any). The When construct can thus be used to programmatically influence which Catch block handles a given error. Note that the When clause is unique to VB.NET. You cannot use a When structure in a Try/Catch block in C# or Managed C++.

Back to Nested Exceptions

Our understanding of exception classes allows us to use nested exceptions very powerfully. You can write an inner Try block that handles only certain errors while you handle the remaining ones in the outer Try block. The advantage of this approach over the single-block technique in Listing 3.13 is that the outer block will also catch any errors generated by the inner block's error handling code:

```
Try
    Try
        'Normal code over here.
    Catch fileError As FileNotFoundException
        'error handling code
    End Try
Catch
    'Catch non-file errors, or errors in the preceding Catch
End Try
```

THROWING EXCEPTIONS

To raise an error in Visual Basic 6 you used Err.Raise. To accomplish the same thing in VB.NET, you throw an exception. It may not seem intuitive, but throwing an exception requires that you first instantiate the appropriate exception class:

```
'Throw a division by zero exception
Dim e As New System.DivideByZeroException()
Throw e
```

HOW AND WHY

Is On Error GoTo Still Part of the Language?

Despite the advantages of structured exception handling, developers can rest assured that VB.NET still supports VB6's traditional On Error Goto mechanism. Note, however, that structured exception handling and On Error Goto are mutually exclusive per function. For each procedure or function you must choose one error handling strategy; you can not intermix the two.

What about the Err object?

Since VB.NET still supports the Err object, you may wonder about the correlation between Err and exception classes. Luckily, VB.NET is smart enough to convert between the two objects. So, if a function throws a `DivideByZeroException`, you can trap it with `Err.Number = 11` (the error code for division by zero). Likewise, if a function raises a file error via `Err.Raise 53`, it will manifest itself to its caller as a `FileNotFoundException`.

SUMMARY

VB.NET now includes structured exception handling constructs similar to those found in C++ and Java. Structured exception handling is implemented using the `Try`, `Catch`, and `Finally` keywords. Program code is placed in a `Try` block, and resulting errors are caught in the `Catch` blocks that follow. Errors in the .NET Framework are differentiated using exception classes, which are special BCL classes that communicate error information.

Structured error handling improves upon VB6's traditional `On Error Goto` mechanism by offering features such as nested exception handling and the `When` keyword, which can programmatically determine which routine handles a given error. VB.NET still supports `On Error Goto`, although you cannot use both techniques in the same function.

Topic: Other Syntax Changes

In this topic we investigate some of the other syntax changes in VB.NET, such as parameter passing, control properties, and File IO. Although subtle, the changes in this chapter can considerably alter the behavior of VB6 code that is ported to VB.NET. For example, VB.NET is much more stringent than VB6 with respect to the scope of variables. Ambiguous code elements such as default properties have been completely removed from this new version of Visual Basic.

CONCEPTS

Parameter Passing

Default Parameter Passing
One of the significant syntax changes in VB.NET is the way in which parameters are passed by default into functions, procedures, and class methods. Consider the following function declaration:

```
Private Function Divide(num As Long, den As Long) As Long
```

In Visual Basic 6, parameters are passed by reference (ByRef) by default. Thus, in VB6, the preceding code is equivalent to the following:

```
Private Function Divide(ByRef num As Long, ByRef den As Long) As Long
```

By passing a parameter by reference, modifications to the parameter are reflected outside the function body. Thus, if Divide() changes the incoming values of either num or den, the changes will persist after the function finishes executing. While this behavior is sometimes intentional, passing parameters by reference often leads to variable values unintentionally changing and other runtime errors that are difficult to debug.

In VB.NET the default parameter passing convention is opposite to that of VB6—by default all parameters are passed by value. In VB.NET, the declaration for Divide() would now be equivalent to the following:

```
Private Function Divide(ByVal num As Long, ByVal den As Long) As Long
```

This protects num and den from modification within Divide. In VB.NET parameters can still be passed by reference, but you must explicitly do so using the ByRef keyword. By making reference parameter passing explicit, developers are more likely to be aware of the dangers of reference passing. In addition, VB.NET's default parameter passing characteristics now comply with those of both C# and managed C++. This conformance is important, because language intermixing is likely to become commonplace in the .NET framework, given the language neutrality of the CLR.

ParamArray Arguments
In VB a procedure or function can accept a ParamArray as its last parameter. A ParamArray is a variable-length array that allows functions to accept a variable number of parameters. You cannot declare the passing mechanism for ParamArray arguments. In VB6 a ParamArray could be passed only by reference. In VB.NET ParamArray can be passed only by value.

Passing Property Parameters by Reference
Recall that a variable passed by reference changes its value if modified by the underlying function. The one exception to this behavior in VB6

occurred when a control property, such as TextBox.Text, was passed by reference. In this case, changes to the variable did not persist outside the function body (it would be as if you passed the variable by value). VB.NET makes things consistent—control properties passed by reference adhere to reference passing semantics:

```
'In VB6, running following line of code does not change
'the contents of the textbox.  In VB.NET, it does.

Modify Text1.Text

Public Sub Modify(ByRef s As String)
    s = "hello world"
End Sub
```

New Arithmetic Shortcut Operators

VB.NET now includes syntax shortcuts found in C++ and Java. These new succinct operators are given in Table 3.2 (although you can still use the older syntax).

VB.NET Shortcut	VB6 equivalent
A += 2	A = A+2
A -= 3	A = A-3
A *= 4	A = A*4
A /= 5	A = A/5
A \= 5	A = A\5
A ^= 6	A = A^6
A &= "some string"	A = A & "some string"

Table 3.2   VB.NET shortcut arithmetic operators

File I/O

Support for VB6's intrinsic file I/O functions continues in VB.NET. The functions Open, Close, Get, Put, Input, and Print are now accessible through the Micrsoft.VisualBasic namespace as FileOpen, FileClose, FileGet, FilePut, Input, and Print, respectively.

You can also perform file I/O in VB.NET using the classes found in the System.IO namespace. A full listing of these classes can be found at VB030006, but Listing 3.15 gives you a brief taste of how they function.

```
Imports System.IO

Module Module1
    'This program uses the stream classes in System.IO to copy
    'the contenst of one file to another.
    Sub Main()

        'Open file and read numbers from a file
        Dim fReader As StreamReader
        Dim fWriter As StreamWriter
        Dim str As String

        'Open file to read:
        fReader = File.OpenText("Numbers.txt")

        'Open file to write:
        fWriter = File.CreateText("Answers.txt")

        'Iterate through the file.
        'Peek will return -1 when the end of the file is reached
        While fReader.Peek <> -1
            str = fReader.ReadLine()
            fWriter.WriteLine(str)
        End While

        fReader.Close()
        fWriter.Close()
    End Sub
End Module
```

Listing 3.15   Using the System.IO classes for file IO

Listing 3.15 copies the contents of one text file to another. The System.IO File class can be used to create, open, copy, delete, and move files. You should recognize that OpenText() and CreateText() are shared members of File (they can be used without creating an instance of the class). These two methods are used to obtain instances of the StreamReader and StreamWriter classes, which can be used to read and write text files, respectively. Note, that the loop construct in Listing 3.15 uses the StreamReader.Peek() method to determine where the file ends (not V6's EOF() element).

Variable Scope

VB.NET changes the visibility of variables within a function. In VB6, a variable, once declared, is accessible throughout the function. In VB.NET, a variable can be referenced only within the code block that defined it. A code block can be a method, function, For Next loop, Do While loop, If Then structure, or Case Select structure. If you are familiar with C++, C#, or Java, you can think of a code block as anything that would ordinarily be contained inside brackets. Listing 3.16 illustrates the difference in behavior:

```
Private Sub Foo()
    Dim i As Long
    For i = 1 To 3
        Dim x As Long
        x = i
    Next i

    x = 5 'Will compile in VB6, not in VB.NET
End Sub
```

Listing 3.16   Variable scope in VB.NET

In VB6, x can be referenced in Foo() anytime after it has been declared. VB.NET changes the language's scoping rules to that of C++ and Java. Thus, x can be referenced only within the block that declared it (the For loop).

The Return Keyword

In VB6, a function returned its value using the following syntax:

```
Function MyFunction() As Integer
    MyFunction = 4
End Function
```

Although you can still use this convention in VB.NET to specify a function's return value, you can accomplish the same thing with the Return keyword:

```
Function MyFunction() As Integer
        Return 4
End Function
```

Properties

VB.NET changes the way in which class properties are both declared and exposed. In VB6, a class declared its properties using the Set, Let, and Get keywords. To expose a numerical property called Age, for example, you would add the following code to a VB6 class module.

```
Private m_Age As Integer

Public Property Let Age(Value As Integer)
    m_Age = Value
End Property

Public Property Get Age() As Integer
    Age = m_Age
End Property
```

Listing 3.17   A class property in VB6

The primary shortcoming of the syntax in Listing 3.17 is that a property has separate blocks of code for its Get and Set logic. VB.NET introduces a unified property declaration scheme by prescribing that all logic be contained within one property block:

```
Private m_Age As integer
Property Age() As String
    Get
        Age = m_Age
    End Get
    Set(ByVal Value As String)
        m_Age = Value
    End Set
End Property
```

Listing 3.18   A class property in VB.NET

Recall that a property in VB6 is set using either the Let or Set constructs (using the former to set a value, the latter to set a reference). Since VB.NET no longer differentiates between setting a variable by reference or value (a change we saw in the first topic on data types), Let and Set have become redundant. The Let keyword has therefore been retired—properties are always set using the Set keyword.

Read-Only and Write-Only Properties

Given the unified property declaration syntax in Listing 3.18, you may wonder how you create a read-only property in VB.NET. In VB6, a property is read only if you omit its `property Set` or `property Let` block. VB.NET makes things clearer through the `ReadOnly` keyword:

```
ReadOnly Property Age() As String
   Get
      Age = m_Age
   End Get
End Property
```

Listing 3.19   A read-only property in VB.NET

Not surprisingly, if you try to include a `Set` block in a `Read-Only` property, VB.NET will raise a syntax error. Note that in VB.NET you cannot write read-only properties in the implicit style of VB6. If you omit the `Set` block in Listing 3.18, VB.NET will throw an error. Closely related to the `ReadOnly` keyword is `WriteOnly`, which makes a property write-only.

Default Properties
In Visual Basic 6, a default property is implicitly used when its object is referenced. Because `text` is the default property of a textbox, the following two statements in VB6 are equivalent:

```
Text1.Text = "hello"
Text1 = "hello"
```

Although default properties make for succinct code, they also make the code more difficult to debug. For example, in the second line of the previous listing, does `Text1` refer to a control or a variable? VB.NET eliminates some of this ambiguity by stipulating that default properties must accept parameters.

In VB6, a default property was created using the Procedure Attributes dialog box. This method of designation was problematic, because you could not tell which property was the default property simply by inspecting code. VB.NET uses the `Default` keyword to make things more explicit:

```
Class SomeClass
   Private m_Age(5) As Integer
   Default Property Age(ByVal index As Integer) As Integer
      Get
         Age = m_Age(index)
      End Get
      Set(ByVal Value As Integer)
```

```
          m_Age(index) = Value
       End Set
    End Property
End Class
```

Listing 3.20   Default properties in VB.NET

Listing 3.20 adds a default property called Ages to our class. Remember that default properties in VB.NET must be parameterized. Therefore, Ages accepts an Integer parameter (the index to the Ages array) and can be used in the following manner:

```
dim sc as SomeClass
sc(1) = 5                'same as sc.Age(1) = 5
```

Of course, we could also claim that the preceding code is also ambiguous. Does sc(1) refer to a default property or to the first element of an array? Even though VB.NET allows default properties with parameters (as illustrated in Listing 3.20), it is best to avoid default parameters entirely, as they can still result in confusing code.

Obsolete Keywords

Many VB6 keywords, functions, and statements have been retired or replaced in VB.NET. Option Base, for example, is no longer supported because all arrays are zero-based in VB.NET. Functions such as Atn, Sgn, and Sqr have been replaced with the Atan(), Sign(), and Sqrt() methods of the System.Math class. Although subsequent chapters highlight many VB6 elements that VB.NET has replaced, a complete list of obsolete keywords can be found at ⟡VB030007.

SUMMARY

In addition to syntax changes, VB.NET also brings about logistical differences from VB6. Variables are no longer passed by reference by default, but instead by value. Variable scope is now more restrictive—a variable can be referenced only within the code block that defined it. Default properties that often result in ambiguous and confusing code must be parameterized. VB.NET also introduces new syntax shortcuts for arithmetic operations, classes for file IO, and the Return keyword to specify a function's return value.

Topic: The VB.NET Upgrade Wizard

Many of the syntax changes described in this chapter are automatically performed by the VB.NET Upgrade Wizard. When you attempt to open a VB6 project in VS.NET, the development environment will automatically invoke the conversion tool shown in Figure 3.1.

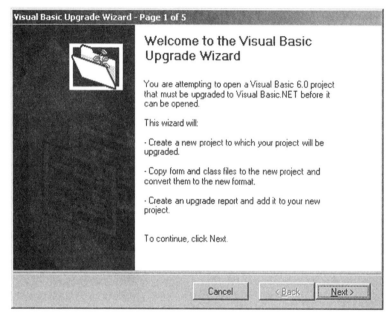

Figure 3.1   The VB.NET Upgrade Wizard

The various screens of the wizard will ask to configure certain aspects of the conversion (where the new VB.NET project should be stored, how certain syntax elements should be treated, etc.). After stepping through these screens the conversion process will begin. During this time the Upgrade Wizard will convert the VB6 elements in your project to their upgraded counterparts. Variant, for example, will be replaced with System.Object. The Set keyword will be removed in object instantiation statements. Of course, not everything can be perfectly converted because some syntax elements do not have direct VB.NET equivalents. In this case, the best the wizard can do is inform you that it encountered a change it couldn't address.

At the end of the conversion process, the Upgrade Wizard will generate a report file detailing its upgrading efforts (as of this writing the file is called _UpgradeReport.htm and is stored in the new project's directory). As depicted in Figure 3.2, the report lists the results of the conversion for each form and module in the project.

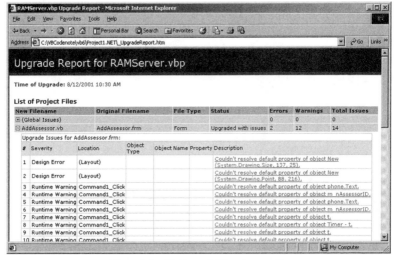

Figure 3.2   VB Upgrade Wizard report file

In addition to the report file, the wizard will also insert comments into the new project's source code:

```
'UPGRADE_WARNING: Couldn't resolve default property of object
'myControl.
myControl = 0
```

It is your responsibility to scour through these comments and manually upgrade code that the wizard couldn't handle. Although conversion will almost always involve some manual effort on your part, the Upgrade Wizard's savvy may surprise you. Consider the following block of VB6 code:

```
Private Sub Command1_Click()
    For i = 1 To 7
        Dim x As Integer
        MsgBox("Test!")
    Next
```

```
    x = 5
End Sub
```

Listing 3.21   VB6 code

From our scoping rules in Listing 3.16, we learned that this syntax is not allowed in VB.NET (a variable cannot be referenced outside the code block where it is defined). In this case, the wizard converted the preceding code to the following:

```
Private Sub Command1_Click(ByVal sender As System.Object, ByVal e
As System.EventArgs) Handles Command1.Click

    Dim i As Object
    Dim x As Short

    For i = 1 To 7
        MsgBox("Test!")
    Next
    x = 5

end Sub
```

Listing 3.22   Code produced by the Upgrade Wizard

As Listing 3.22 illustrates, the wizard moved the declaration of x to the the top of function so that it could be accessed outside the For loop (note that x is now a Short in agreement with Table 3.1). Also note, that the i variable that was used without declaration in VB6 is now explicitly declared as an Object. Finally, observe that the Command1_Click method is now considerably more complex than its VB6 version in Listing 3.21. We explain the new event handler syntax when we look at Windows Forms in Chapter 7.

SUMMARY

When you are converting code from VB6 to VB.NET, the Upgrade Wizard can take care of a remarkable amount of the drudgery. However, the Upgrade Wizard can go only so far. You will still have to look through the autogenerated comments (search for "UPGRADE_WARNING" in your code). You will also have to pay attention to the language changes mentioned earlier in this chapter and native code (see Chapter 8).

Chapter Summary

VB.NET fundamentally changes many elements of the VB6 syntax.

- The Variant data type has been replaced with the more capable Object. In addition to being able to store any data type in VB.NET, objects are classes and expose methods such as ToString() and GetType().
- You no longer use Set when instantiating objects.
- VB.NET includes new data types such as Decimal and Char. All
- VB.NET data types map to some equivalent in CTS (Integers to System.Int32, booleans to System.Boolean, etc.).
- Custom types are defined using Structure, not Type.
- VB.NET strings map the System.String class. The methods of this class can be used for common string operations. VB6 string functions such as Mid(), and Left() are still supported.
- Fixed-length strings (dim s as string *100) are no longer supported. Use Char arrays instead.
- VB.NET arrays are always zero-based; the To and Option Base keywords are no longer supported.
- Option Strict On is a directive that instructs VB.NET to disallow implicit casting for hazardous assignments.
- In addition to using VB6 style collections, you can use the new collections in the System.Collection namespace. Use these collections when interfacing with languages such as C# and managed C++.
- In addition to using On Error Goto, you can use VB.NET's new structured exception handling features to trap errors. Structured exception handling uses the Try/Catch/Finally keywords found in Java and C++, and it is more flexible than the older On Error mechanism.
- Default properties must be parameterized. This stipulation avoids ambiguous code such as Text1 = "Happy" (which is equivalent to Text1.Text = "Happy").
- VB.NET includes shortcut arithmetic operators such as a+=3, which is equivalent to a=a+3.
- In addition to VB6's file IO functions such as Open(), Close(), and Print(), you can use the stream classes found in the System.IO namespace to read and write to files.
- A function (MyFunction()) can return a value using the Return keyword (Return 3) as opposed to creating a variable with the same name as the function (MyFunction = 3).

• Function variables can be referenced only within the code block that defined them. In VB6, a variable, once declared, was globally accessible throughout the function.

Chapter 4

—

NEW VB.NET CONCEPTS

VB.NET introduces two new concepts to the world of Visual Basic: object inheritance and threading. Although both of these features were available in a limited fashion in VB6, they are now a native part of the language.

If you have worked with other languages, you may be familiar with the concept of *object inheritance,* which allows classes to inherit the behavior of other classes. Class inheritance is an important concept when working with the BCL. For example, you may extend many aspects of the .NET Framework (e.g., custom exceptions) through class inheritance.

VB.NET's second new feature is *threading.* Threading allows applications to have multiple streams of execution so they can do many things at once. High-performance applications often use threads that perform complex tasks while still responding to user events. As this chapter illustrates, the increased versatility of threading comes at a cost—most notably the safety concerns that threads raise.

VB.NET's inclusion of object inheritance and threading into the language makes it considerably more powerful than its predecessors. In the enterprise setting, VB is frequently used as a front-end tool, whereas more capable languages such as Java and C++ do the real work. VB.NET levels the playing field considerably. This chapter illustrates that it, too, can be used to create powerful applications and components.

Topic: New OOP Features

Whether Visual Basic qualifies as a true object-oriented language is subject to debate. Although VB6 contains core OOP concepts such as classes, it lacks some of the more sophisticated features found in Java and C++. VB.NET puts much of this debate to rest by introducing advanced OOP elements such as polymorphism, behavioral inheritance, and native interfaces. Class inheritance, for example, allows you to inherit the structure *and implementation* of other classes. Interfaces form contracts between clients and components by prescribing which methods a class must expose. As illustrated in this topic, VB.NET is now a powerful development tool for object-oriented development.

CONCEPTS

No More Class Modules

Programming with classes in VB6 required adding class modules to your project. If you have an application with 10 classes, your VB project must have 10 separate class files. With VB.NET a single source file can contain multiple classes:

```
Public Class A
    Public Sub Hello1()
        Console.WriteLine("Hello1")
    End Sub
End Class

Public Class B
    Public Sub Hello2()
        Console.WriteLine("Hello2")
    End Sub
End Class

Module Module1

    Sub Main()
        Dim myA As New A()
        Dim myB As New B()
        myA.Hello1()
        myB.Hello2()
```

```
    End Sub

End Module
```

Listing 4.1   Multiple classes in a source file

The ability for one source file to contain numerous classes makes projects easier to manage and distribute. If, for example, you have a collection of classes that perform financial calculations, you can group them in a single file for distribution.

Interfaces

Interfaces are best understood by considering VB6's Implements keyword. If a VB6 class A Implements another class B, it must provide implementations for all the methods defined in B. Consider a class called Calc with methods Add() and Subtract(). For a second class Foo Implements Calc, VB6 stipulates that Foo must implement the Add() and Subtract() methods.

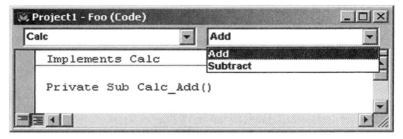

Figure 4.1   The Implements keyword in VB6

As Figure 4.1 illustrates, the Implements keyword is contractual—any class that implements Calc must contain Add() and Subtract() methods (of course, it can also expose additional methods such as PrintAnswer() or GetTime()).

Remember, however, that Calc itself is a class and can be used directly by clients. In VB6 we must thus use one class to define the requirements of another. VB.NET interfaces also allow you to prescribe the methods a class must expose, but in a more intuitive and explicit manner.

Interfaces in VB.NET

Interfaces in VB.NET exist for the sole purpose of defining which methods a class must implement. As such, interfaces can only contain method (sub and function) prototypes—they cannot contain implementations themselves. Listing 4.2, for example, provides an interface for a simple two-function calculator:

```
Public Interface ICalc
    Sub Add(ByVal x As Integer, ByVal y As Integer)
    Sub Subtract(ByVal x As Integer, ByVal y As Integer)
End Interface
```

Listing 4.2   ICalc interface

Interface names are usually prefaced with a capital *I* (a practice that derives from VB6's underlying architecture, COM). Notice that neither method has an End Sub tag. Because of the Interface keyword, VB.NET knows that the interface contains only method prototypes. The compiler will prevent you from adding any implementation inside this code.

Implementing an Interface
Once you have an interface defined as in Listing 4.2, you can implement it in a separate class file. To implement an interface, simply add the Implements keyword after the declaration of your class. Similar to VB6, the methods defined in the interface will automatically appear in the VS.NET's upper right window, as shown in Figure 4.2.

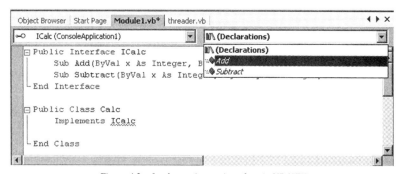

Figure 4.2   Implementing an interface in VB.NET

You must provide an implementation for every method defined in the interface. To implement ICalc (Listing 4.2), for example, you could use the following:

```
Public Class Calc
    Implements ICalc
```

```
    Sub Add(ByVal x As Integer, ByVal y As Integer) _
        Implements ICalc.Add
        Console.WriteLine("{0} + {1} = {2}",x, y, x + y)
    End Sub

    Sub Subtract(ByVal x As Integer, ByVal y As Integer) _
        Implements ICalc.Subtract
        Console.WriteLine("{0} - {1} = {2}",x, y, z - y)
    End Sub

End Class
```

Listing 4.3   Implementing the interface

Notice that each class method must explicitly identify which interface method it is implementing. For example, the `Subtract()` method implements `ICalc.Subtract`. This notation provides an extra cross-check for the compiler.

The implementation class is not restricted only to the methods defined in the interface. We could easily modify the `Calc` class to include a new `Square()` method:

```
Public Class Calc2
  Implements ICalc
  'Add and Subtract methods are identical to Listing 4.3
  Sub Square(ByVal x As Integer)
    Console.WriteLine("{0} ^ 2 = {1}", x,x*x)
  End Sub
End Class
```

Listing 4.4   Adding extra methods

Multiple Interfaces

A single class can implement multiple interfaces. However, the class must provide an implementation for each method in each interface. We might, for example, create a second calculator interface defining additional scientific methods:

```
Public Interface IScientific
    Sub Cosine(ByVal x As Integer)
End Interface
```

Listing 4.5   IScientific interface

We could create a scientific calculator by implementing both interfaces:

```
Public Class SciCalc
    Implements ICalc, IScientific

  Sub Add(ByVal x As Integer, ByVal y As Integer) _
      Implements ICalc.Add
    'Same as Listing 4.3
  End Sub
  Sub Subtract(ByVal x As Integer, ByVal y As Integer) _
      Implements ICalc.Subtract
    'Same as Listing 4.3
  End Sub
  Sub Cosine(ByVal x As Integer)  _
      Implements IScientific.Cosine
    Dim z As Double
    z = System.Math.Cos(x)
    Console.WriteLine("COS({0}) = {1}", x, z)
  End Sub
End Class
```

Listing 4.6   Implementing multiple interfaces

You might wonder what occurs if two interfaces contain a method with the same name and signature. In this case, the explicit link to the interface method becomes important. If IScientific in Listing 4.5 also contained an Add() method, we could implement both Add() methods in the SciCalc class as follows:

```
Public Class SciCalc
    Implements ICalc, IScientific

  Sub Add_1(ByVal x As Integer, ByVal y As Integer) _
      Implements ICalc.Add

  End Sub

  Sub Add_2(ByVal x As Integer, ByVal y As Integer) _
      Implements IScentific.Add

  End Sub
End Class
```

Listing 4.7   Two interfaces with the same method

In this case Add_1() provides the implementation for ICalc's Add(), and Add_2() provides the implementation for IScientific's Add(). We could also implement both Add()'s with one function in the derived class as follows:

```
Public Sub Add(ByVal x As Integer, ByVal y As Integer) _
    Implements ICalc.Add, ICalc2.Add
    'implementation
End Sub
```

Polymorphism, Part 1
One aspect of interfaces that was not apparent in VB6 is the concept of *polymorphism.* Polymorphism is the ability to treat the implementation class as an instance of itself or as an instance of the interface (we will expand this definition in the second Polymorphism section in this chapter).

```
'Crate instance of Calc (Listing 4.3)
Dim myCalc as new Calc
myCalc.Add()

'Create Calc, and cast to ICalc (Listing 4.2)
Dim i_Calc as new ICalc
i_Calc = New Calc
i_Calc.Add()
```

Listing 4.8   Casting a class to an interface

Listing 4.8 illustrates two techniques to call the Add() method. The first code block simply calls the Add() method against an instance of Calc. The second block casts Calc to an ICalc interface before also calling Add(). For those unfamiliar with the term, to *cast* means to convert an object to one of its parent types.

The second technique may not seem especially useful. After all, why not simply call methods against an instance of the class itself and avoid the extra step of casting to an interface? The point is that by casting to an interface, we can access only the methods defined in the interface—we cannot access other methods the class may have defined. This is important for two reasons.

First, an interface can serve as a protection mechanism. We might, for example, append a method to the Calc class called BeCareful() that is intended only for privileged clients. By giving unauthorized clients an ICalc interface instead of Calc, we prevent them from calling BeCareful() while still allowing them to invoke Add() and Subtract().

A second, more pragmatic use of interface casting is illustrated in

Listing 4.9. This listing contains a method called AddNumbers(), which accepts an ICalc interface as a parameter.

```
Public Class PolyMorphism
  Sub AddNumbers(calculator as ICalc)
    'class performs add function, using any class
    'that implements ICalc:
    calculator.Add(5, 4)
  End Sub

  Sub main()
    'create an instance of Calc, cast to ICalc and
    'call AddNumbers():
    Dim i_calc as ICalc
    i_calc = New Calc
    AddNumbers(i_calc)
  End Sub
End Class
```

Listing 4.9   Polymorphism in action

In Listing 4.8, we call AddNumbers() by first casting an instance of Calc to ICalc. Alternatively, you can just pass in an instance of Calc, and VB.NET will cast it implicitly. The main point of Listing 4.9 is that AddNumbers() does not care about the underlying class—it will accept *any* class that implements the ICalc interface. We could just as easily replace the Calc class with the scientific calculator we created in Listing 4.6 by replacing the bold lines with the following:

```
Dim i_calc as ICalc
i_calc = New SciCalc()
AddNumbers(i_calc)
```

Listing 4.10   An alternative calculator

The AddNumbers() method will still work because the SciCalc class (Listing 4.6) also implements ICalc. Remember, however, that because AddNumbers() accepts an ICalc interface, it can call only Add() and Subtract(). It cannot call Cosine(), even though this method is implemented by the scientific calculator class.

Inheritance

Inheritance is a classic computer science concept that has been specifically omitted from Visual Basic up until VB.NET. In short, inheritance is simply code reuse. Almost every nontrivial project will involve situations in which two or more classes have overlapping functional requirements. Rather than repeat identical code in all of the classes (creating a maintenance nightmare), you can create a class with the common functionality (often called the *base class*). The specialized classes can *extend* (inherit from) the base class, thus inheriting the common functions. If the common code has to change, it can be changed in the base class without modifying the specialized classes.

Through the use of inheritance, you can create a class that builds on (inherits) the functionality of another (base) class. You can further specialize the class by replacing (overriding) some functionality of the base class. Inheritance allows a second form of polymorphism whereby a specialized class can act just like the parent class in certain situations but completely different in others.

Every programming language that incorporates inheritance has a slightly different set of rules. VB.NET is no exception. If you are familiar with inheritance in C++ or Java, you will find that VB.NET uses different keywords and slightly different assumptions than these other languages.

Inheritance and VB.NET
With VB.NET, you can inherit the behavior of any class. It is important to realize that inheriting behavior means inheriting implementation code. Reusing the calculator example from Listing 4.3, we can create a basic calculator class (Listing 4.11) and extend the class to create a scientific calculator (Listing 4.12).

```
Public Class Calc
  Public Function Multiply(ByVal x As Integer, _
      ByVal y As Integer) as Integer
    Return x*y
  End Function
End Class
```

Listing 4.11   The base calculator class

When we create the scientific calculator, we can inherit the base calculator methods by using the Inherits keyword in the class definition:

```
Public Class SciCalc Inherits Calc
  Public Sub Factorial (ByVal x As Integer)
    Dim z as Long
    z = 1
    if (x > 1) then
      for i = 1 to x
```

```
      z = Multiply(z, i)
    next i
  end if
End Sub
End Class
```

Listing 4.12   Scientific calculator

Because `SciCalc` inherits from `Calc`, the `Factorial()` method automatically has access to the `Calc.Multiply()` method. The `SciCalc` class does not have to implement methods for the basic `Calc` functions, because they are included through inheritance.

Overriding a Method
In some cases, the base-class method isn't exactly correct for the derived class. The derived class may need to override (or replace) the base-class method. In VB.NET, base-class methods cannot be overridden unless they are specifically identified with the `Overridable` keyword. That is, by preceding a function declaration with `Overridable`, you are giving derived classes permission to replace the function. We can modify the base calculator by adding the following `Subtract()` method:

```
Public Class Calc
    Public Overridable Function Subtract( _
        ByVal x As Integer, ByVal y As Integer) As Integer
        Console.WriteLine("Calc's Subtract")
        Return Math.Abs(x - y)
    End Function
    Public Function Multiply(ByVal x As Integer, _
        ByVal y As Integer) As Integer
      Return x * y
    End Function
End Class
```

Listing 4.13   An overridable method

Derived classes still inherit the implementation of `Overridable` functions, so any call to `Subtract()` will use the code in Listing 4.12. `Overridable` becomes significant only when the derived class replaces the implementation of the base class. Those familiar with C++ can think of the `Overridable` keyword as roughly equivalent to the `virtual` keyword.

As can be seen from Listing 4.13, `Calc.Subtract()` method disallows negative results (perhaps because it assumes mathematically naive clients). Since a scientific calculator is bound to have more sophisticated users, it can replace this limited implementation with its own version using the Overrides keyword:

```
Public Class SciCalc inherits Calc
    Public Overrides Function Subtract( _
        ByVal x As Integer, ByVal y As Integer) As Integer
      Console.WriteLine("SciCalc's Subtract")
      Return x - y 'allow negative numbers!
    End Function

  Public Sub Factorial (ByVal x As Integer)
        'Same as listing 4.11
  End Sub
End Class
```

Listing 4.14   Overriding a method

If you create an instance of SciCalc and call Subtract(), the more capable code in Listing 4.14 will be used.

Polymorphism, Part 2
Similar to interfaces, you can cast a derived class to its base type. A function that expects a Calc class (Listing 4.13), for example, would also accept a SciCalc class (Listing 4.14). The combination of Overridable functions and class casting leads to a second, more accurate definition of polymorphism that we now examine.

Notice that the Subtract() method for each class (Listings 4.13 and 4.14) prints out a different message to the console. Consider the following code, which casts an instance of SciCalc to a Calc class and then calls Subtract().

```
Sub Main()
  dim Answer
  Dim myCalc as Calc
  myCalc = new SciCalc()
  Answer = myCalc.Subtract(6,4)
```

Listing 4.15   Polymorphism

In this case, which version of Subtract() gets called? (And hence, what will the output on the console be?) There are two lines of reasoning:

1. Since we dimensioned myCalc as a Calc, Calc's version of Subtract() gets executed and the program prints "Calc's Subtract."

2. Even though `myCalc` was dimensioned as `Calc`, it was cast to an instance of `SciCalc`, so `SciCalc`'s `Subtract()` is called and the program outputs "SciCalc's Subtract."

Those of you who reasoned out (or guessed at) the second answer are correct. VB.NET is smart enough to figure out at runtime that `Calc` is really a scientific calculator, and `SciCalc`'s implementation gets called. In other words, a call to an overridden method will always result in the derived implementation, regardless of how the class is referenced. This leads to a more accurate definition of polymorphism: *the dynamic binding of method invocations to a particular class.*

All this definition says is that in Listing 4.15, VB.NET determines which `Subtract()` gets called at *runtime*. This is because it can be established only at runtime whether `Calc` points to a `Calc` class or to a derived class, `SciCalc`.

The Shadows Keyword

Situations may arise when you don't want the dynamic behavior of the `Overrides` keyword. That is to say, you want the derived function to be called only when a program specifically references the derived class type. This is accomplished by substituting the `Shadows` keyword for the `Overrides` keyword in Listing 4.14.

```
Public Class SciCalc inherits Calc
   Public Shadows Function Subtract( _
       ByVal x As Integer, ByVal y As Integer) As Integer
       Console.WriteLine("SciCalc'c Subtract")
       Return x - y 'allow negative numbers!
   End Function

 Public Sub Factorial (ByVal x As Integer)
       'Same as listing 4.11
 End Sub
End Class
```

Listing 4.16   Overriding a method

If you run the code in Listing 4.15 now, it will call the base class's method and print out "Calc's Subtract."

System.Object

In Chapter 3 we pointed out that the `System.Object` data type has supplanted VB6's `Variant`. Our understanding of class inheritance allows us to state the following axiom in the .NET Framework:

Every data type derives from System.Object.

Thus, inheritance is performed implicitly whenever you create a class, structure, or even primitive data type (Integer) in VB.NET. By imposing this rule on all data types in the .NET Framework, the CLR ensures that they will always support the methods of Object. One of these methods, for example, is called Finalize() and is called by the CLR's garbage collector. As explained in Chapter 6, an object that wishes to be notified of its collection must implement its own Finalize() method using the Overrides keyword:

```
Public Class SomeClass
    'Use Finalize instead of Class_Terminate
    Protected Overrides Sub Finalize()
        'If our object had allocated resources, it would
        'release them here.
    End Sub
End Class
```

Listing 4.17   Overriding System.Object.Finalize()

In Chapter 3 we also pointed out that you could use an Object when you were unsure of a variable's contents at compile time:

```
Sub MyGenericFn(s as Object)

    'Do something

End Sub
```

Note that MyGenericFn() can accept *any* data type in VB.NET. Because of the axiom we have stated, VB.NET can cast whatever variable MyGenericFn() receives into an Object.

Inheritance in VB.NET
The previous chapter illustrated VB.NET's new structured exception handling capabilities. In that topic we saw that you could trap errors in VB.NET with the following line (placed within a Try block):

```
Catch unknownError As Exception
```

In Chapter 3 we explained that errors in the .NET Framework are represented using exception classes. A divide-by-zero exception is caught using a DivideByZeroException class, whereas a file-not-found error is signified through the `FileNotFoundException` class. As you may have guessed, all exception classes inherit from the base `Exception` class. Thus, the preceding line of code will catch all errors in the .NET Framework.

You can also write your own custom exception class by inheriting (and extending) the base `Exception` class. In fact, the .NET Framework exposes much of its functionality through class inheritance. To enable certain properties of a web service component that can be accessed over the Internet (Chapter 9), your class must inherit from `System.WebService`. Another common use for inheritance is *Visual Inheritance,* a technique that allows you to design a form and inherit the properties of the form (the controls it contains, etc.) into other forms. Visual Inheritance is covered in Chapter 7.

Inheriting across Languages
Chapter 5 explains that VB.NET can inherit classes written in C#, managed C++, or any other language capable of producing IL code. Likewise, classes you write in VB.NET can be inherited in other languages. Cross-language inheritance is a very powerful capability that is likely to make language intermixing in the .NET Framework commonplace.

HOW AND WHY

How Do I Prevent a Class from Being Inherited?
To prevent a class from being inherited, declare it with the `NotInheritable` keyword:

```
Public NotInheritable Class Calc
```

You can also specify that a class must inherit from another class using the `MustInherit` keyword. In this case you are telling VB.NET that the class cannot be directly instantiated by clients—it can be derived only by other classes. See ⟨CN⟩VB040004 for more on these keywords.

How Do I Prevent a Method from Being Inherited?
To prevent a method from being inherited by derived classes, declare it with the `Private` keyword. The method will be visible only within the class and cannot be accessed by derived classes or clients. Alternatively, you may want to give only derived classes (not clients) the ability to call a method. In this case, precede the method declaration with the `Protected` keyword. The method will be callable only from the base class and derived classes.

SUMMARY

VB.NET introduces two powerful new OOP constructs that make it a viable tool for object-oriented development—interfaces and object inheritance.

An *interface* is a collection of function prototypes that serves as a contract between a client and component. By implementing an interface, a class guarantees that it supports certain methods. Interfaces can be explicitly defined in VB.NET, allowing for a form of polymorphism whereby a class can cast itself to one of the interfaces it has implemented. The polymorphic behavior in VB.NET allows clients to use interfaces without regard to the class that implements them.

VB.NET now includes *object inheritance,* which is the ability of a class to inherit the functions and implementation code of another class. Inheritance is useful in situations where two or more classes have intersecting functionality. By placing common code in one class (called the *base class*), and inheriting it across other classes (called *derived classes*), changes to the base class are immediately reflected in the derived ones.

Inheritance can become tricky when a derived class replaces the implementations for methods of a base class. VB.NET introduces three keywords to deal with this situation:

1. `Overridable`   Used by a base class to denote that a method's implementation can be replaced by a derived class. Similar to the `virtual` keyword in C++.
2. `Overrides`   Used by a derived class to indicate that it is replacing the base class's implementation. Stipulates that the new implementation is called even if the derived class has been cast to the base class.
3. `Shadows`   Also used by a derived class to indicate that it is replacing the base class's implementation. The new implementation is called, however, only if the method is executed directly on the derived class. If the derived class is cast to the base class, the original implementation gets called.

Topic: Threading

This topic examines the double-edged world of threading—double-edged because, although threading gives the developer increased latitude and flexibility, it also brings with it a host of new concerns. In VB6 you were abstracted from threading by the VB Runtime. It is true that VB6 applications could use threads via the Windows API `CreateThread()` function, but this was not a straightforward process. The BCL classes found in the `System.Threading` namespace make threads natively accessible from VB.NET.

The concepts of threads are best understood in terms of the VB6 application depicted in Figure 4.3.

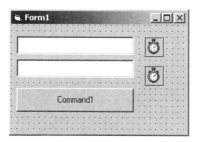

Figure 4.3   VB6 timer application

The application in Figure 4.3 contains two `Timer` controls, `Timer1` and `Timer2`; two textboxes, `Text1` and `Text2`; and a command button, `Command1`. Recall that a `Timer`'s `Interval` property determines how often its associated code executes (in milliseconds). By setting `Timer1.Interval` to 100 and `Timer2.Interval` to 500, we are instructing VB6 to run `Timer1`'s code every tenth of a second and `Timer2`'s code every half second. Also, by setting the `Enabled` property of both timers to `False`, we ensure that the timers don't begin executing when the application is started.

Add the following code to your project, which uses each `Timer` control to update a `TextBox` with successive numbers. Note that we have used VB6's `Val()` function to convert the contents of the `TextBox` (a string) into a number.

```
Private Sub Command1_Click()
    Timer1.Enabled = True
    Timer2.Enabled = True
End Sub

Private Sub Timer1_Timer()
    Text1.Text = Val(Text1.Text) + 1
End Sub
```

```
Private Sub Timer2_Timer()
    Text2.Text = Val(Text2.Text) + 1
End Sub
```

Listing 4.18   VB6 timer source code

Run the VB6 timer application and you will observe the effect of giving each timer a different Interval property—one textbox increments faster than the other. The point to note is that our VB6 application appears to be doing two things at once (incrementing each textbox). In other words, the application has two streams of execution. This is all a thread is—a stream of execution within your program. If a program has multiple threads, it can, like our VB6 timer application, appear to do numerous things at once.

Threading is useful when a program has operations that must be performed in unison. When you print a document in Microsoft Word, for example, it starts a separate printing thread so that it can still respond to your keystrokes (this is called *printing in the background*). When you request a web page, the browser uses threads for communication so that it can incrementally render the information it receives. Applications with more than one thread are said to be *multithreaded.*

Thread Classes

The .NET Framework exposes classes for threading in the System .Threading namespace. The primary class in this namespace is, appropriately, called Thread, and you use it to create threads in your VB.NET applications. Threads are best illustrated by the following example, which uses a thread-based approach to achieve the same functionality as our VB6 timer application.

Threading Example

In this example we will rewrite the VB6 timer application using threads. To begin, create a Windows Application project in VS.NET. Next, drag two textboxes and a button onto the form so that it resembles Figure 4.4.

We explore the new Windows Forms controls in Chapter 7, but note that VS.NET gives the button a default name of Button1—not Command1—as was the default in VB6. Similarly, the first textbox assumes the name TextBox1 instead of Text1. Double-click Button1 and add the following code to your project (lines in bold are automatically generated by VS.NET).

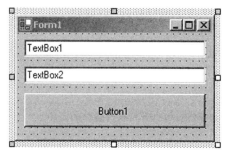

Figure 4.4   VB.NET threading application

```
Imports System.Threading 'don't forget this!

Public Class Form1
    Inherits System.Windows.Forms.Form

+Windows Form Designer generated code 'explained in Ch 7

    Private Sub Button1_Click_1(ByVal sender As _
        System.Object, ByVal e As System.EventArgs) _
        Handles Button1.Click

        'Create two threads to update the textboxes:
        Dim oThread1, oThread2 As Thread
        oThread1 = New Thread(AddressOf UpdateText1)
        oThread2 = New Thread(AddressOf UpdateText2)
        oThread2.Start()
        oThread1.Start()

    End Sub

    'Starting Point for Thread number1
    Sub UpdateText1()
        Do
            TextBox1.Text = Val(TextBox1.Text) + 1
            'delay for 1 second:
            Dim t = Timer : Do : Loop Until Timer - t > 1
        Loop
    End Sub

    'Starting Point for Thread number2
    Sub UpdateText2()
        Do
```

```
            TextBox2.Text = Val(TextBox2.Text) + 1
            'delay for 0.1 seconds:
            Dim t = Timer : Do : Loop Until Timer - t > 0.1
        Loop
    End Sub
End Class
```

Listing 4.19   VB.NET threading code

First note that we had to import the System.Threading namespace to use the Thread class in Listing 4.19. The Thread class is used by the button's click event (Button1_Click), which spawns both threads in the application. When instantiating a Thread class you must tell it where the new thread will begin its execution. This requires that you specify a function (or class method) using VB's AddressOf operator:

```
oThread1 = New Thread(AddressOf UpdateText1)
oThread2 = New Thread(AddressOf UpdateText2)
```

The preceding two lines do not start threads, but they create two Thread objects that will begin their execution at UpdateText1() and UpdateText2(), respectively. If you look in Listing 4.19, you will see that these two functions update Textbox1 and Textbox2, albeit at different rates. To explicitly start both threads, we must call the Thread class's Start() method, as illustrated in Listing 4.19.

Note that unlike the Timer controls in our VB6 application, the Update functions are not repeatedly invoked by the system. By spawning a thread you are merely pointing it to function where it begins executing. When the function exits, the thread dies. To achieve the same functionality as the Timer controls in our VB6 application, we must place our counting code within a loop and perform our own delay using VB's Timer() function (recall that Timer() returns the number of seconds past midnight).

If you run the application by pressing F5 and clicking Button1, you will observe behavior similar to the VB6 timer application—both textboxes update simultaneously, one faster than the other. The difference from the VB6 application is that we have used threads explicitly for our concurrent operations. Note that once you click Button1, the application actually has *three* threads running. In addition to the two threads explicitly created, the application has an *initial* thread created by VB.NET. It is this thread that creates the form and textboxes, responds to our button clicks, and so on. Every application has at least one (initial) thread. Threading is a powerful capability and is particularly useful when your application must perform operations in parallel. Like most things, however, increased latitude comes at a cost.

Thread Safety and Time Slicing

To understand thread safety, we must understand that a thread is merely an abstraction for an uglier, more complicated reality. At its most basic level, a computer's processor can do only one thing at a time (yes, some machines have multiple processors, but this discussion also applies to them). This limitation is a problem for the Windows operating system because it wants to do many things at once (Windows is a *multitasking* OS). For example, it wants to allow our application to update both textboxes concurrently.

Windows must compromise with the processor's restrictions. Since the processor can do only one thing at a time, the operating system allows each thread in an application to run for a given duration. When time expires, another thread is allowed to execute—and so on. The interplay between Windows and the VB.NET application in Listing 4.19 might look something like this:

```
Windows (3:00:00pm): Thread 1, GO.
Thread1: TextBox1.Text = 1,2,3,4,5,6,7,8,
Windows (3:00:05pm): Thread 1, STOP.  Thread 2, GO.
Thread2: TextBox2.Text = 1,2,3,4,
Windows (3:00:10pm): Thread 2, STOP, Thread 1, GO.
Thread1: TextBox1.Text = 9,10,11....
```

By shifting between threads at an incredible pace (a process called *time slicing*), Windows maintains the illusion that our application is doing many things at once. Remember, however, that at any given moment only one thread in the application is running. Thus, while the application in Listing 4.19 seems to be updating both textboxes at once, it is actually interchanging between both operations very quickly.

Time Slicing Example

To see the effects of time slicing, create a console project in VS.NET and insert the following code into the module that is automatically created for you (Module1).

```
Public Class MathLib
    'we will use the following variable in the next example:
    Private Shared pbase As Integer
    Shared Function Power(base As Integer, exp As Integer) As Long
```

```
      Return base ^ exp
   End Function
End Class

Sub Main()
   Dim oThread1, oThread2 As Thread
   oThread1 = New Thread(AddressOf Function1)
   oThread2 = New Thread(AddressOf Function2)
   oThread1.Start()
   oThread2.Start()
End Sub

Sub Function1()
   Do
      Console.WriteLine("[Thread1]:2^3 = {0}", MathLib.Power(2, 3))
   Loop
End Sub

Sub Function2()
   Do
      Console.WriteLine("[Thread2]:3^4 = {0}", MathLib.Power(3, 4))
   Loop
End Sub
```

Listing 4.20   Time slicing example

Listing 4.20 works in a manner similar to the previous example—it creates and starts two Thread objects that perform different operations. Both threads repeatedly call the Power() method of the MathLib class we have written (also in Listing 4.20). Note that Power() is a *shared* method, which, as we learned in Chapter 1, means that we can call it without first instantiating the class. It may seem odd that we have written an entire class to calculate exponents, but this is necessary for the next example on thread safety.

Run the application in Listing 4.20 and you will see the effects of time slicing—Windows will switch back and forth between each thread:

```
[Thread1]: 2^3 = 8
[Thread1]: 2^3 = 8
[Thread2]: 3^4 = 81
[Thread2]: 3^4 = 81
[Thread1]: 2^3 = 8
[Thread1]: 2^3 = 8
```

```
[Thread2]: 3^4 = 81
[Thread2]: 3^4 = 81
```

Listing 4.21   Time slicing output

You can influence how Windows time-slices each thread using the `Priority` property of the `Thread` class. For example, to specify that `Thread1` should be given more execution time than `Thread2`, you would add the following lines to Listing 4.21 (before the `Start()` methods).

```
'ThreadPrority is an enumeration in System.Threading.
oThread1.Priority = ThreadPriority.AboveNormal
oThread2.Priority = ThreadPriority.Normal
```

Run the modified application and you will see that `Thread1` is given a majority of the execution time. The `Priority` property is useful when certain operations are more important than others. A thread that is printing in the background, for example, would probably be given a lower priority than a thread responsible for real-time updates on the screen.

Back to Thread Safety

You may wonder what any of this has to do with safety. The problems arise specifically because of time slicing. Just as a thread can switch in and out of its execution states, so, too, can any function it calls. If a function is being used by multiple threads (such as the `Power()` method in Listing 4.20), it must be prepared for the possibility that it can be interrupted at some point during its execution, only to be awoken at another, different, point.

To witness the dangers of threading, replace the implementation of the `Power()` method in Listing 4.20 with the following code:

```
'inside MathLib class
shared Function Power(base as integer,
                      exp as integer) as Long
   dim k as integer
   pBase=base
   for k=1 to exp - 1
      pBase*=base
      'delay for two seconds inside the function
      dim t as double = timer
      do: loop until timer - t > 2
   next
return pBase
end Function
```

Listing 4.22   Unsafe thread code

Instead of using VB's intrinsic ^ operator, Listing 4.22 calculates exponents using a For loop that repeatedly multiplies the base number by itself (to calculate 2^3, the function would perform 2 × 2 × 2). We will explain the presence of the 2-second delay inside the method in a moment. If you run the application with the modified Power() function, you might be surprised to see the following output:

```
[Thread1]: 2^3 = 162
[Thread2]: 3^4 = 4
[Thread1]: 2^3 = 54
[Thread2]: 3^4 = 24
[Thread1]: 2^3 = 9
[Thread1]: 2^3 = 72
```

Listing 4.23   Unsafe application output

To understand what is going on, look back at the Power() method in Listing 4.22. To calculate an exponent, the method stores the base in a private class variable called pBase. Since this variable is used by the Power() method to service both threads, consistency problems arise. Consider once again the interplay between Windows and our application:

```
Windows: Thread 1, GO.
Thread1: pbase = 2. 2^3 = pbase[2] *
Windows: Thread 1, STOP.  Thread 2, GO.
Thread2: pbase = 3. 3^4 = pbase[3] * pbase[3] *
Windows (3:00:10pm): Thread 2, STOP.  Thread 1, GO.
Thread1: ... * pbase[3] = 2^3 = (2x2x3) = 12
```

Consider the execution of Listing 4.22 carefully. Windows begins by telling Thread1 to execute. Thread1 calls the Power()method, which calculates 2^3 by first setting pBase to 2. The method then enters the For loop, but before the method can finish, Windows switches execution to Thread2. Thread2 also calls Power(), which now sets pBase to 3. At some point, Thread1 awakes and continues its operation inside the For loop. *The problem is that pBase is no longer 2, as Thread1 expects, but 3.* As a result, we get the unpredictable results in Listing 4.23.

The delay in Listing 4.22 assures us that a thread switch occurs inside Power()'s For loop, which leads to the behavior just described. If you remove the delay from Listing 4.22 and run the application, you will still see inconsistent results, but not as often. It may take thousands of iterations, but eventually the timing will be such that Power() will fail. This illustrates one of the more lethal aspects of thread safety problems—they can be very difficult to detect. A program may run successfully for days until eventually certain conditions give way to the problem. Reproducing the problem (and hence debugging it) is very difficult given its sporadic nature.

Thread Safety Protection

The .NET Framework includes several classes in the System.Threading namespace to combat thread safety problems. One of these classes is called SyncLock, which is used to create a *critical section* in your code—a section that cannot be interrupted with a thread switch. As the following code illustrates, we can use this class to rectify the problem with the Power() method.

```
Public Class MathLib
  Private Shared pbase as Integer
  Dim Shared myLock As String = "" 'MUST initalize!


  Shared Function Power(base As Integer, exp As Integer) As Long
        'Enclose the entire function within SyncLock.
        'The code must now run to completion before a
        'thread switch occurs.
     SyncLock myLock
        Dim k As Integer
        pBase=base
        For k=1 To exp - 1
           pBase*=base
           Dim t As Double = Timer
           Do: Loop Until Timer - t > 2
        Next
        Return pBase
     End SyncLock
  End Function
End Class
```

Listing 4.24   A thread-safe Power() method

Listing 4.24 uses the SyncLock class to place the entire method within a critical section. Note that SyncLock requires a *reference* variable (Chapter 3 discusses reference and value types) for internal purposes. Thanks to SyncLock, the entire Power() method will execute uninterrupted. Run your application and you will see consistent results.

The amount of code in a critical section should be kept to a minimum.

Remember, during a critical section a thread switch cannot occur. If you place a lengthy routine within a critical section you are preventing other threads in your application from being serviced.

You may think that thread safety is as simple as placing all your methods within SyncLocks. Unfortunately, this is not the case. For example, if two threads interact with each other, a situation can arise where each one is waiting for the other to complete a task. This recursive dependency is known as *deadlock* and must be avoided at all costs. If you proceed into the world of threading, you must concern yourself with concepts such as causality, reentrance, and race conditions. Indeed, thread safety is a complicated subject. A full discussion of the topic and its nuances would consume several CodeNotes books. For more information, see ⊶VB040001.

The .NET Framework exposes features with which you can make an entire class thread-safe (i.e., synchronize access to all of the thread's methods). This is accomplished by using the Synchronization attribute (attributes are discussed in Chapter 6) found in the System.EnterpriseServices namespace. There are several performance issues with this technique, however, and it is generally not recommended. For details see ⊶VB040002.

HOW AND WHY

How Many Threads Should I Use in My Application?
There is no definitive answer to this question, but realize that the more threads you have in an application, the harder Windows has to work to switch between them. Using several threads can cause significant overhead and synchronization problems.

A common practice is to have one thread that responds to user events and one or more threads that perform lengthy operations when required. Since VB.NET automatically creates a thread for user events, this translates into using threads only for operations that must be performed in parallel. For a more detailed discussion on thread use in VB.NET, please see ⊶VB040003.

SUMMARY

Threads allow an application to have multiple streams of execution so that it can appear to do many things at once. VB.NET applications create threads using the Thread class in the System.Threading namespace.

To create a thread, you must provide it with the function where it begins executing.

Applications that use multiple threads must guard against thread safety problems. These problems are a result of time slicing—a process in which Windows rapidly runs each thread for a small amount of time so they appear to operate simultaneously. Additional classes in System.Threading provide tools to address the thread safety problem. One such class is called SyncLock, which allows a section of code to execute without interruption from Window's thread switcher.

Chapter Summary

VB.NET introduces two fundamentally new features into the VB environment. Object inheritance allows classes to inherit the behavior of other classes, whereas threading allows VB applications to have multiple streams of execution. In the minds of many developers, these features remove two of the last great obstacles separating Visual Basic from other "real" languages such as C++ and Java.

Object inheritance in all of its forms will rapidly become part of the vocabulary for any VB.NET programmer. It will be very difficult to write a VB.NET program without using some form of inheritance. In fact, as you will see in Chapter 7 (Window Forms), it is impossible to write a GUI without inheriting from a base Form class. Once developers are exposed to the mandatory forms of inheritance required to use the language, the power of using object-oriented programming will become readily apparent.

Similarly, now that threading is available, most developers will have a hard time resisting the temptation to write multithreaded Visual Basic applications. However, no matter how simple the syntax, using threads is always a complicated task. Keep in mind that adding threads to an application must be done with great care, as threads can induce a large set of problems, from race conditions to deadlocks. In the end, however, adding threads to VB provides much greater program control than was previously available.

Chapter 5

—

ASSEMBLIES

As we learned in Chapter 1, applications developed with VB.NET will run only on those computers with the .NET Framework installed. This makes sense, because VB.NET programs are compiled to Intermediate Language (IL) code, which is interpreted on the fly by the Common Language Runtime (CLR). Without the CLR, a VB.NET application is merely a dormant file on your hard drive, as there is no entity to make sense of the application's contents. Thus, if you attempt to run the `HelloWorld.exe` application we created in Chapter 1 on a .NET-less machine, you will receive an error telling you that `mscoree.dll` (the system file where the CLR lives) cannot be found.

In addition to containing IL code, .NET executables and component files (EXEs/DLLs) also contain *metadata,* which describes the types (classes, structures, constants, etc.) that these files expose. In fact, .NET EXEs and DLLs have changed so much in the .NET Framework that Microsoft has given them a new name: *assemblies.*

In this chapter we cover the two fundamental aspects of application development in the .NET Framework: assemblies and metadata. In the first topic, we illustrate the virtues of metadata by writing a class in C# and then extending it in VB.NET. In the second topic, we see how assemblies solve the problem of "DLL Hell" through the CLR's use of public key cryptography.

Topic: Assemblies and Metadata

This first topic will introduce you to the basic structure of assemblies and metadata. As mentioned previously, an assembly is similar to a DLL, but the tools used to build an assembly are significantly different.

CONCEPTS

Tangent: Calling the Windows API from VB6

To understand the role of metadata in the .NET Framework, let us examine an important capability in Visual Basic 6: calling the Windows API. VB developers frequently use the Windows API for functionality that transcends the language. Among other things, the Windows API contains functions for low-level file IO, high-granularity timing, and interesting graphical effects (see Chapter 7) that may not be directly accessible from VB. This example also serves as a good reference for Chapter 8, where we illustrate how to leverage the Windows API from VB.NET.

Calling the Windows API from Visual Basic 6 is often a cumbersome process because the API is intended primarily for C and C++ developers. In addition to familiarizing yourself with the idiosyncrasies of the functions you use, you must account for the complex parameters they accept (a *complex* parameter is a type that is not intrinsically supported by VB). Throughout this example, make note of the provisions we must make for using complex types. As we will see, the difficulties we encounter in this example quickly dissipate through .NET's use of metadata.

Consider the `GlobalMemoryStatus` API function that can be used to determine the amount of memory in the system. To use this function in VB6, you must add a module to your project and insert the following function declaration into the module (remember, this is VB6, not VB.NET—to add a module you must use VB6's "Add Module" menu option):

```
Public Declare Sub GlobalMemoryStatus Lib "kernel32" _
  (lpBuffer As MEMORYSTATUS)
```

For those unfamiliar with API declarations, the preceding line informs VB6 that the `GlobalMemoryStatus` function resides in the `kernel32.dll` system file. When `GlobalMemoryStatus` is called from within a program, the VB Runtime loads `kernel32.dll` and invokes the function appropriately. For this reason, a function declared in such a manner is sometimes referred to as an *external function,* as its implementation code is housed outside the Visual Basic environment.

Look closely at the preceding function declaration and you'll see that GlobalMemoryStatus accepts a parameter whose type is foreign to Visual Basic—MEMORYSTATUS. Unlike an Integer or Double, VB6 does not know what a MEMORYSTATUS variable looks like. In order to educate VB so that it can understand and use a nonnative data type, we must explicitly define the MEMORYSTATUS type by adding the following code to the module:

```
Public Type MEMORYSTATUS
   dwLength As Long
   dwMemoryLoad As Long
   dwTotalPhys As Long
   dwAvailPhys As Long
   dwTotalPageFile As Long
   dwAvailPageFile As Long
   dwTotalVirtual As Long
   dwAvailVirtual As Long
End Type
```

Listing 5.1   Defining the MEMORYSTATUS type

As a result of the type definition in Listing 5.1, we can use GlobalMemoryStatus to determine the amount of RAM on the system:

```
Dim mem As MEMORYSTATUS

'The following line populates the "mem"
'variable with system information:
GlobalMemoryStatus mem

'display amount of RAM on the system
MsgBox mem.dwTotalPhys
```

Listing 5.2   Calling an API function from VB6

The important point to note is that the GlobalMemoryStatus function (or more accurately, the kernel32.dll file that houses it) has no way of communicating the parameter details in Listing 5.2 to our application. We must obtain the type definition of MEMORYSTATUS manually, either by looking in the Windows API documentation or by using the API viewer utility that comes with VB6. Furthermore, because many API functions accept parameter types that cannot be represented in VB (such as C/C++

pointers), they cannot be called even if their parameter information is known.

Enter Metadata and Assemblies

The previous example illustrates two problems when trying to communicate between Visual Basic 6 and the Windows API domain (the world of C/C++):

1. C++ and VB6 do not agree on permissible data types and the representation of those types. Thus, certain functions authored in C++ cannot be called from VB6.
2. A component cannot communicate its own type information to a client. Thus kernel32.dll couldn't give us the layout of the MEMORYSTATUS structure—we had to determine it manually.

.NET solves both of these problems. The first problem is overcome by Common Type System (CTS) discussed in Chapter 1. Because the CTS defines all of the permissible types in the .NET Framework, VB.NET, C#, and managed C++ all agree on the representations for basic data types such as integers and strings. Developers can construct complex types (such as the MEMORYSTATUS structure in Listing 5.2), but they will always be made up of the basic types defined by the CTS.

The second problem is addressed through metadata, which is the universal format used to describe types in the .NET Framework and is embedded into every .NET component. As we will see, metadata is used to store more than just type information. It is the format used to house a component's security, versioning, and dependency information. It is used by the CLR to ensure that components run against the proper resources and that they have the proper security requirements to carry out the functions they perform.

IntelliSense and COM

A powerful feature in Visual Basic 6 is IntelliSense, whereby a list of methods appears whenever you press a period following an object in the VB6 environment. After selecting the particular method you wish to call, the VB6 environment also lists all the parameters the method expects. VB6's underlying component architecture, COM, gives rise to this functionality. Behind the scenes, the VB environment queries the COM component for type information, which it then displays in an intuitive manner via IntelliSense.

The problem with COM (in addition to the versioning problems illustrated in the next topic) is that version and type information are stored in two different places: the registry and a type library (which is usually embedded as a resource in the component itself). .NET eliminates the need to keep component information in two locations—the metadata for a .NET component is stored entirely within the component itself. .NET components are thus self-describing in that they contain both IL code and all of the necessary information needed to execute it. This glorified component has been a given a new physical structure in the .NET Framework, as well as a new name—the *assembly*.

Assemblies Defined

An assembly is the new way that executable code is packaged and deployed in the .NET Framework. What makes an assembly special is not the metadata it contains, but simply that the CLR can interpret it in some useful manner. For example, the CLR uses metadata to accomplish the following:

1. Ensure that an assembly's methods are called in a type-safe manner
2. Ensure that an assembly runs against the proper versions of other assemblies it may depend on (the Shared Assemblies topic later in the chapter illustrates this)
3. Determine and provide other runtime requirements of the assembly

Although assemblies are still usually stored inside DLLs and EXEs, a single assembly can span multiple files (called *modules* in .NET). An assembly could, for example, span three modules. The first module could contain IL code; the second could contain resources such as bitmaps and sounds; and the third could contain the metadata that glues them together. For this reason, an assembly is more accurately referred to as a *unit of deployment* rather than a self-contained component.

Why Metadata?

The presence of type-describing metadata in an assembly allows you to inherit a class from a compiled .NET component *as if it were an intrinsic class written in VB.NET itself.* Reflect on what this means for a moment. You can inherit both the interface and behavior of classes written in managed C++ or C#. Similarly, classes authored in VB.NET are instantly accessible from any other language in the .NET Framework. This language-neutral versatility arises from .NET's introduction of the CLR and CTS.

EXAMPLE

To illustrate the premise behind assemblies and metadata, we will write a class in C# which, like the GlobalMemoryStatus function in Listing 5.2, uses a complex structure. We will then extend and call the class from VB.NET. If you don't know the C# language, don't worry, this example is very straightforward. The source for this example can also be found online at CN⟩VB050001.

Consider the C# class given in Listing 5.3.

```csharp
using System;

namespace MathClass
{

public struct Dimension
{
    public float Height;
    public float Width;
};


public class MathCS {

        public float AreaRectangle(Dimension d)
        {
        return d.Width * d.Height;
        }

}
}
```

Listing 5.3   C# mathematical class

The MathCS   class in Listing 5.3 exposes one method called AreaRectangle, which returns the area of a rectangle whose dimensions are specified using the Dimension structure (also defined in Listing 5.3). The implementation of AreaRectangle is trivial—it simply calculates the area of the rectangle by multiplying the rectangle's width by its height.

Notice that Listing 5.3 contains no Main() method. The .NET Framework allows one to create *library assemblies*. Unlike an application, a library assembly does not execute but simply exposes a collection of types. Those of you familiar with ActiveX will find the library concept similar to an ActiveX component that exposes a collection of classes to clients. Also notice from Listing 5.3 that both the MathCS and Dimension types are enclosed within the MathClass namespace. As we will see, we will need to use this namespace to access these types from the subsequent VB.NET application.

Save Listing 5.3 into a file called MathLib.cs and compile it from the command line using the C# compiler. Invoke the command prompt using the VS.NET Command Prompt icon, as illustrated in Chapter 2 (Figure 2.5), and execute the following command:

```
csc.exe /t:library MathLib.cs
```

The C# compiler will produce a library assembly called MathLib.DLL. Note that you could also write a library assembly using the VS.NET IDE—an approach we will examine in the Shared Assemblies topic, when we write a library assembly in VB.NET.

The ILDASM Utility

The Mathlib.DLL file produced by the C# compiler is not an ordinary Win32 DLL but an assembly that contains IL code and self-describing metadata. To look at this metadata, we can use a tool provided by Microsoft called ILDASM.EXE, which allows us to inspect the makeup of a given assembly. Developers familiar with ActiveX or COM will find ILDASM similar to the OLEVIEW.EXE tool, which allows them to examine the internals of a COM component.

Go to the directory where Mathlib.DLL is located and execute the following command:

```
ILDASM /adv Mathlib.DLL
```

ILDASM (an acronym for Intermediate Language Disassembly) will load the assembly and bring up a screen similar to the one depicted in Figure 5.1.

As can be seen from Figure 5.1, ILDASM gives the breakdown for both the Dimension structure and the MathCS class (which are both contained within the MathClass namespace). Note that the Dimension structure consists of two float variables in accordance with Listing 5.3. Likewise, the AreaRectangle method accepts one dimension parameter, also in agreement with Listing 5.3.

You can also use ILDASM to examine the metadata that was generated by the C# compiler by going to its View menu and selecting Metadata → Show! The metadata listing is quite verbose, but looking through it you will find the following definition:

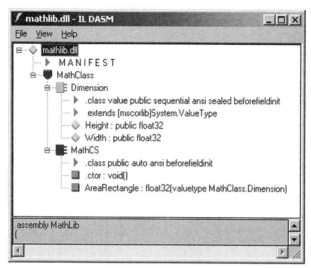

Figure 5.1   Using ILDASM to inspect an assembly

```
TypeDef #1
-----------------------------------------------------------
     TypDefName: MathClass.Dimension   (02000002)
     Flags      : [Public] [SequentialLayout] [Class] [Sealed]
[AnsiClass]  (00100109)
     Extends    : 01000001 [TypeRef] System.ValueType
     Field #1
     -----------------------------------------------------------
          Field Name: Height (04000001)
          Flags      : [Public]  (00000006)
          DefltValue:
          CallCnvntn: [FIELD]
          Field type:  R4


     Field #2
     -----------------------------------------------------------
          Field Name: Width (04000002)
          Flags      : [Public]  (00000006)
          DefltValue:
          CallCnvntn: [FIELD]
          Field type:  R4
```

Listing 5.4   The metadata for the dimension structure

Listing 5.4 shows the metadata for the Dimension structure that we defined. It is this metadata that allows other IL languages to use the structure. Note the [Public] specifier in the Flags section of the metadata, meaning that all clients can see and use the Dimension structure. If you scan through the rest of the listing, you will also find metadata for the MathCS class, as well as other boilerplate compiler insertions that we examine momentarily.

Using the Assembly
The presence of Dimension's type information inside MathLib.dll has important implications. Unlike the previous Windows API example, we don't have to manually define a complex structure in Visual Basic to use a method or function that utilizes complex types. Instead, complex type definitions are automatically imported by VB.NET by reading the assembly's metadata. Thus, a VB.NET program that uses the AreaRectangle method is extremely straightforward. First create a new Console project in VS.NET called VBCall. Next, reference the C# assembly we just created by going to Project → Add Reference → Browse and select MathLib.DLL from the directory in which it is located. The MathLib assembly is now referenced by your project, which you can verify by looking in the Solution Explorer window (see Figure 5.2).

Figure 5.2   Referencing the MathLib assembly in VS.NET

Having referenced the assembly, we can now add the code in Listing 5.5 to our project, which uses the C# class that we wrote.

```
Imports MathClass 'Must import this namespace to use C# class.

Module Module1
    Sub Main()
        'The dimension type is automatically imported
        'by VB.NET:
```

```
dim mySize as Dimension
dim myCS as MathCS
myCS = new MathCS()

'Set the dimensions of the rectangle whose area we
'we wish to find:
mySize.Width = 10
mySize.Height = 5

Console.Writeline("Area of Rectangle: {0}", _
    myCS.AreaRectangle(mySize))
    End Sub
End Module
```

Listing 5.5   A VB.NET program that calls the MathCS class

Run the application by pressing F5. It will inform you that rectangle of width 10 and height 5 has an area of 50 units. Note that we must *import* the MathClass namespace defined in Listing 5.3 to use the MathCS class.

As can be seen from Listing 5.5, we don't have to define the Dimension data type—the VB.NET compiler automatically obtains its definition from MathLib.DLL. Such seamless interoperability is a virtue of the self-describing nature of assemblies—they contain all the type information needed to call their members.

Look closely at Listing 5.5 and you will notice that we had to explicitly instantiate the MathCS class using new(), whereas the Dimension structure was instantiated implicitly (we simply needed to declare it). Remember from our discussion in Chapter 3 that a class is a *reference* type and thus must be explicitly allocated, whereas a structure is a *value* type that is allocated implicitly when it is declared.

Extending the C# Class

Remember that an assembly consists of language-independent IL code. It is thus possible to inherit and extend the C# class in VB.NET. The following VB.NET code extends the MathCS class through a second class called MathVb, which adds a method called AreaEllipse(). As its name suggests, AreaEllipse calculates the area of an ellipse given its dimensions.

```
Imports MathClass

Class MathVB: Inherits MathCS

    Public Function AreaEllipse(d As Dimension) As Double
```

```
            Return d.Width * d.Height * Math.PI * 0.25
    End Function
End Class

Module Module1
    Sub Main()
        Dim mySize As Dimension
        Dim mVB As MathVB
        mVB = New MathVB()

        mySize.Width = 10
        mySize.Height = 5
        Console.Writeline("Area of Rectangle: {0}", _
          mVB.AreaRectangle(mySize))
        Console.Writeline("Area of Ellipse: {0}", _
          mVB.AreaEllipse(mySize))

    End Sub
End Module
```

Listing 5.6   Extending the C# class

Insert the preceding code into a new VS.NET Console project named VBExtend. As in the previous example, don't forget to reference the MathLib.DLL assembly once you have created the project. As can be seen from Listing 5.6, the AreaEllipse method returns the area of an ellipse given its dimensions (the area of an ellipse is given by the formula $\frac{1}{4}\pi \times$ width $\times$ height). Note that to obtain the value of π we used the BCL Math class found in the System namespace.

Run the Console application and you will see that the area of an ellipse is smaller than that of a rectangle with similar dimensions:

```
Area of Rectangle: 50
Area of Ellipse: 39.2699081698724
```

Examining the VB Application's Metadata

Remember that the application produced from Listing 5.6 is not a standard Win32 application but an assembly packaged in executable format. As we did with the MathLlib.DLL, we can use the ILDASM tool to examine the metadata of the VB.NET application. VS.NET stores the application executable in your project's bin directory (\someDiectory\VBExtend\bin\). Navigate to this directory from the command line and then execute the following:

```
ILDASM /adv VBExtend.exe
```

Inspect the application's metadata by going to View → Metadata → Show! and you will find that the metadata for the MathVB class contains the following line:

```
Extends    : 01000001 [TypeRef] MathClass.MathCS
```

The metadata reflects what we expect: the MathVB class extends the MathCS class. Look elsewhere in the metadata and you will find the following:

```
AssemblyRef #3
-------------------------------------------------------
        Token: 0x23000003
        Public Key or Token: <null>
        Name: MathLib
```

The AssemblyRef section of the metadata contains the assembly's dependency information. This section of metadata allows the CLR to determine that when the VB.NET application is executed, the C# assembly that we wrote (MathLib.dll) is required and should be automatically loaded.

The Manifest

The section of metadata that contains the configuration and dependency information of the assembly is called the *manifest*. You can examine the manifest by clicking on the MANIFEST icon shown in Figure 5.1. Doing so brings up a textual representation of the manifest that is shown in Listing 5.7 (certain parts of it have been omitted for brevity).

```
.assembly extern mscorlib
.assembly extern Microsoft.VisualBasic
.assembly extern System
.assembly extern System.Data
.assembly extern System.Xml
.assembly extern MathLib
.module VBExtend.exe
// MVID: {0737DB24-1BAF-4EE5-BCD7-7450160B819C}
```

Listing 5.7   An assembly's manifest

As illustrated in Listing 5.7, our VB.NET application depends on numerous other assemblies. In addition to the assemblies that are automatically referenced by VS.NET (such as `mscorlib` that contains the core BCL classes found in the `System` namespace and `Microsoft.VisualBasic` that houses intrinsic VB6 elements), our assembly, `MatLib`, is also referenced. As one might expect, `MathLib` is included in the application's manifest because we explicitly added it as a reference to our VS.NET project.

Also recall that assemblies can consist of multiple modules. This allows an assembly to span its contents across multiple files (one module could contain program code and the second program resources). The manifest contains a list of the modules that constitute the assembly (in our case only `VBExtend.exe`), as well as the Module Version IDs (MVIDs) that uniquely identify them.

From this example we can see the seamless cross-language communication that the CLR facilitates. We wrote a class in C#, which was extended and used in VB.NET. It is important to realize that we could have extended a class written in any .NET language, be it C#, managed C++, or even VB.NET itself. We could have also done the reverse. That is, we could have authored a class in VB.NET and extended it in C#.

HOW AND WHY

What Would Have Happened Had We Omitted the "namespace MathClass" Line in the C# Program in Listing 5.3?

Namespaces are not required under the .NET Framework. Rather, they are meant to organize your classes in a hierarchical fashion, prevent name collisions with other classes, and simplify access in general. If we had omitted the `MathClass` namespace in our C# listing, then we could also have omitted referencing the namespace in our VB program and still accessed the C# class. Namespaces are simply a syntactical suggestion, but a convention you should follow if others will be using your components.

What Is the Relationship between an Assembly and a Namespace?

An assembly is a unit of deployment, whereas a namespace is a scope for type definition. An assembly houses executable code; a namespace prevents name collisions and makes code more readable. A single assembly can contain multiple namespaces. If you wrote an assembly to expose mathematical functions, for example, you might partition your code into standard and scientific services and group them into two namespaces called `MyCalc.Standard` and `MyCalc.Scientific`.

Can I Prevent a Class from Being Inherited by Other Programs?

Look at Listing 5.3 and you will see that the `public` keyword precedes the declaration of the `MathCS` class. The `public` extension advises the C# compiler that this structure should be visible to all programs that attempt to access this component. With .NET, one can specify the visibility of types to the outside world. The public extension is the most lenient specification, allowing access to all who want it. There are four other visibility extensions that can be used:

- `private`   Stipulates that a class's method can be called directly only by the class itself.
- `protected`   Stipulates that a class's method can be called only by the class and derived classes.
- `friend` and `protected friend`   These two extensions require an understanding of concepts explored in the Shared Assemblies topic of this chapter. Details of these two keywords can be found at ⟿VB050002.

To make a class inaccessible to the other programs, you would precede its declaration with either the `private` or `protected` keywords.

SUMMARY

Assemblies are the new file format used to house executable code in the .NET Framework. Assemblies can span multiple modules (files) and are more accurately thought of as "units of deployment" than as traditional components. Assemblies are self-describing, as they contain information about the types they expose as well as any dependency information. This self-describing information is stored in a binary format called *metadata,* which one can inspect using the ILDASM utility.

Because assemblies are compiled into language-independent IL code, their data types can be seamlessly inherited (and used) by any .NET language. This means that VB.NET can inherit classes written in C# and managed C++. Similarly, classes written in VB.NET can be used by other .NET languages.

Topic: Shared Assemblies

Assemblies, like DLLs, are often meant to be shared between developers. This topic introduces the concept ot a shared assembly and illustrates techniques used to properly version and sign an assembly. As you will see in this topic, shared assemblies go a long way toward eliminating the problem of the profusion of mismatched DLLs that has plagued so many development efforts.

CONCEPTS

The DLL Hell Problem

Microsoft has touted the assembly as the end of the "DLL Hell." To understand the significance of this claim, we must recognize why the problem of DLL Hell arose in the first place. The idea behind the dynamic link library (DLL) was that applications could share components for common and useful routines. Consider the Windows API application that we wrote in Listing 5.2. There, we used the GlobalMemoryStatus function located in the kernel32.dll system file to determine the amount of RAM on the machine. By using a function that was already exposed by the operating system, we didn't have to write a similar function manually. And, because kerner132.dll is a globally accessible library, other applications can also use the numerous functions it exposes (including GlobalMemoryStatus). By sharing executable code, applications are smaller, consume less hard drive space, and can take advantage of new DLL versions without recompilation.

Problems arise with the DLL model because it becomes difficult to impose a versioning scheme for shared libraries. Developers frequently update shared DLLs, unaware (or unconcerned) that numerous other programs depend on them. Consider what would happen if another developer installed a new version of kernel32.dll on the system—one where the GlobalMemoryStatus function accepted two parameters instead of just one. As a result of this incompatible upgrade, our program in Listing 5.2 will no longer work. Similarly, other applications that have made assumptions about the contents of kernel32.dll may also be thwarted.

COM/ActiveX

Microsoft's Component Object Model (COM) promised to eradicate DLL Hell by imposing a strict versioning policy for components. The premise behind COM was that a component's interface (its methods signatures), once published, could never change. Thus, if a developer wrote a component containing a `GlobalMemoryStatus()` method that accepted one parameter, he or she was forbidden from changing the method's signature. By adhering to such a restriction, developers could guarantee that clients would always run against compatible components.

Although COM was a step forward, it wasn't perfect. If you have used COM components from VB6 (e.g., ActiveX controls or ActiveX components), you may recognize the errors shown in Figure 5.3.

Figure 5.3   COM versioning problems

Quite often, these errors arise when a COM component is incompatible with its previous version. You might wonder how this is possible, given that COM stipulates that interfaces are never to be changed once published. This constraint, however, is voluntary. Developers can (and frequently do) change published interfaces, breaking compatibility with older components. If you develop ActiveX components with VB5 or VB6, you may also encounter such errors if you fail to properly set the Version Compatibility option in your project (for details see ᴄᴺ▸VB050003).

Assemblies
With .NET, Microsoft has finally eliminated the problem of DLL Hell through assemblies. As with COM, the assembly infrastructure employs a versioning scheme to prevent developers from updating components in such a way as to break compatibility. Unlike COM, versioning is enforced through public key cryptography—a rigorous security model that is arguably impossible to foil. Thus a developer cannot, either through ignorance or malice, upgrade a component to change its behavior without special permissions and key-based information. There are two types of assemblies under the .NET infrastructure: private and shared.

Private Assemblies
Private assemblies are not designed to be shared. They are designed to be used by one application and must reside in that application's directory or subdirectory. This isolated methodology is nostalgically reminiscent of the DOS days when applications were fully contained within their own directories and did not disturb one another. By default, all as-

semblies (like the one we created in the previous example) are private. If you wish to make them shared, you must explicitly do so by *signing* them, as the upcoming example will illustrate. It is expected that the majority of assemblies you create will be of the private type.

Shared Assemblies

For those components that must be distributed, Microsoft offers the shared assembly. The shared assembly concept is centered around two principles. The first, called *side-by-side execution,* allows the CLR to house multiple versions of the same component on a single machine. The second, termed *binding,* ensures that clients obtain the version of the component they expect. Together, these two principles free developers from having to ensure that their components are compatible with earlier versions. If a component evolves through versions 1.0, 1.1, and 2.0, the CLR will maintain separate copies of each version and invoke the correct one accordingly.

Security and the Global Assembly Cache

What differentiates the shared assembly model from COM or Win32 DLLs is that the versioning policy is not voluntary or based on considerate programming practices, but is enforced through public key cryptography. A full discussion of cryptography and its use by the Common Language Runtime would quickly plunge us into the cryptic world of hashing, tokens, digital signatures, and other topics beyond the scope of this book (see ⟨CN⟩VB050004 for a full discussion). These subjects can quickly become overwhelming, but you need only understand that to enforce versioning, the CLR must ensure the following:

1. Shared assemblies can be updated only by authorized parties.
2. If a component is updated and is incompatible with its predecessor, clients expecting the older version receive it.

These requirements are facilitated by two entities. The first is a *private key* that you obtain to sign an assembly, allowing you (and only you) to update it. The second is the Global Assembly Cache (GAC), which can house multiple copies of a shared assembly based on your signature and the version information used to build it. This information (signature and version) is stored in the manifest of all clients who wish to access the assembly, allowing the CLR to load the appropriate version at runtime. Shared assemblies are best illustrated through the following example.

EXAMPLE

Shared Assembly
In this example we will consider the evolution of hypothetical component called MathLib, a library assembly that exposes mathematical
functions. MathLib is a rather limited library, as it exposes only one
function. Specifically, MathLib exposes a function called Factorial(),
which client applications can use to calculate the factorial of a number.

In order to deploy Mathlib as a shared assembly, we first create a private key using the SN.EXE utility that ships with the .NET Framework
(to call this utility you must invoke the command prompt using the
VS.NET Command Prompt icon shown in Chapter 2, in Figure 2.5):

```
SN.EXE −k MathLib.snk
```

This line of code instructs SN.EXE to store a globally unique private key
into a file called MathLib.snk (private key files in the .NET Framework
end with the snk extension). The term *globally unique* means that our
key is guaranteed to be different from any other key created by another
individual (or subsequent keys that we might generate). It is very important that we keep the private key in our sole possession. If someone
else gained access to Mathlib.snk, they could produce assemblies that
looked like they were authored from us.

Now that we have generated a private key, we can author our shared
assembly. Create a VB Class Library project in VS.NET named Math-
Lib, and add the following code to the project's Class1.vb file:

```
Public Class MathClass
   Public Function Factorial (num As Integer) As Integer
      Dim nAnswer,k As Integer

      For k = 1 To num
         nAnswer = nAnswer * k
      Next
      Console.WriteLine("Factorial v1.0.0.0")
      Console.WriteLine("{0}! = {1}",k,nAnswer)
      Return nAnswer
   End Function
End Class
```

Listing 5.8   The MathLib library

To make our assembly shared, we must first associate it with the private key we created. Right-click on your project in the Solution Explorer

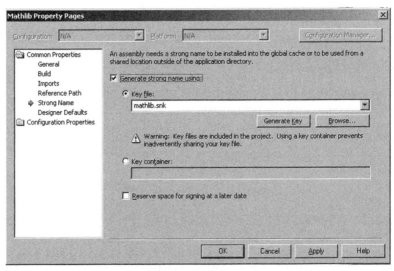

Figure 5.4   Signing the assembly

toolbox and select Properties. Now click Strong Name under Common Properties, which will bring up the screen shown in Figure 5.4.

VS.NET gives you two options with respect to the project's private key. You can either specify a private key file that you generate explicitly using SN.EXE, or you can let VS.NET generate one for you by clicking the Generate Key button. As illustrated in Figure 5.4, use the browse button to select the Mathlib.snk key file we generated.

Next you must give your assembly a version number. When we created the project, VS.NET appended a file to our project called AssemblyInfo.vb. Look inside this file (by clicking it in the solution explorer), and replace the following line:

```
<Assembly: AssemblyVersion("1.0.*")>
```

with this line:

```
<Assembly: AssemblyVersion("1.0.0.0")>
```

The preceding line is an *attribute,* which is a nonprogrammatic statement that influences code generation. Attributes are covered in detail in Chapter 6. We explain the effect of modifying this line momentarily, but understand that our actions thus far inform VS.NET that this is version 1.0.0.0 of the assembly and that it will be signed with the key contained in Mathlib.snk.

Build the project by selecting Build from the VS.NET's Build menu, and you can now deploy the MathLib.DLL file produced by VS.NET as a shared assembly. Behind the scenes, VS.NET embeds the private key located in Mathlib.snk into the assembly itself, where it can be used for security and versioning purposes. Before we consider how a client would install and use MathLib.DLL, a few words must be said about the versioning scheme used in the .NET Framework.

Versioning and Compatibility

Look at the second highlighted line in Listing 5.8. Notice that we have given our assembly a version number of 1.0.0.0. This information is embedded into the manifest of MathLib.DLL. Version information in the .NET Framework takes on the following form:

```
<major version>.<minor version>.<build number>.<revision>
```

The first two sections (major and minor), are referred to as the *incompatible portions* of the version number, whereas the last two (build and revision) are called the *compatible portions*. When a new version of a component is released, if its major or minor number changes, it is deemed incompatible with its predecessor. If the build or revision number changes, however, it is considered compatible with its older variants. If there are two compatible versions of a component on the same machine, the default behavior of the CLR is to give a client the one with the latest build and revision numbers.

Thus, if a client is built against version 1.0.0.0 of our component, and we release version 1.0.1.1, the CLR assumes the two are compatible and will give the client the component with the latest build and revision numbers (in this case v1.0.1.1). If however, we release version 1.5.0.0, the CLR will assume the versions are incompatible, and older clients will receive v1.0.0.0.

Keep in mind that this versioning scheme is a suggested nomenclature. The CLR has no way of ensuring that version 1.0.1.1 of our assembly is backward compatible with its predecessor. Because we are the only ones who possess the private key, however, we need not worry about a third party releasing an assembly that falsely claims to be compatible with ours. The private key security afforded by the CLR assures us that if we follow its versioning scheme, clients will be running compatible versions of *our* code.

Given the described nomenclature, you may be confused with the 1.0.* version number that VS.NET initially assigned our component. When you place an asterisk after the major and minor numbers, you are telling VS.NET to automatically assign build and revision numbers to your component according to the following rules:

- Build number will be equal to the number of days since January 1, 2000, local time.
- Revision number will be equal to the number of seconds since midnight local time, divided by 2 (86,400 seconds in a day = 43,200 possible rev numbers per day).

This means that every successive compilation of our assembly will have different build and revision numbers, provided, of course, that you don't recompile faster than once every 2 seconds. Such a rapidly changing versioning scheme is useful in development and testing scenarios where you may be rebuilding a component many times and will want to test a client against the latest component. It is not appropriate for client deployment, however, which is why we changed the version number from 1.0.* to 1.0.0.0.

In addition to specifying the version number of an assembly, you can optionally specify its culture, which can be used when you are deploying multilanguage assemblies. We will not use it in our example here, but you may consult ⟨CN⟩VB050005 for details.

Deploying the Shared Assembly

Having released v1.0.0.0 of our shared assembly, suppose Jessica the student wishes to use it. She downloads it from our website. Next, she must register it in her computer's Global Assembly Cache (GAC) using a utility called GACUTIL.EXE. (Remember, the Global Assembly Cache houses multiple versions of the same assembly.)

```
GACUTIL.EXE /i MathLib.DLL
```

Alternatively, we could have written an installation script and the Windows Installer, version 2.0 or greater would have registered the shared assembly automatically (for details on how to do this see ⟨CN⟩VB050006).

As a result of running GACUTIL.EXE (or by running an installation script that invoked the utility behind the scenes), the assembly is now registered and copied into Jessica's Global Assembly Cache, which she can view by using the Windows Explorer and inspecting the \%Winroot%\Assembly directory. Navigating to this area invokes the Assembly Cache Viewer, which is a shell extension that provides a friendly view of all the shared assemblies on the system. (A shell extension is a component that extends some aspect of the Windows user interface, such as the Windows Explorer.) This is shown in Figure 5.5.

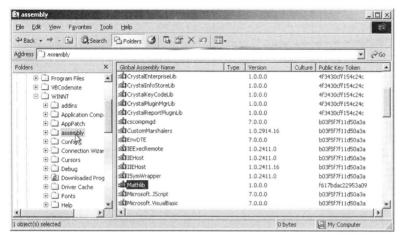

Figure 5.5   The Assembly Cache viewer

Next to our component, we see the version number and something called the *public key token*. The public key token can be thought of as a portion of our private key that assures Jessica that any MathLib.DLL updates she receives will be from us. We revisit the public key token momentarily, when we consider how the assembly is updated.

Pleased that she will no longer have to compute factorials by hand, Jessica writes a VB Console application in VS.NET to use our library. (Remember, however, that because of the language neutrality of the CLR, her client application could have been written in any .NET language.) Before writing her program, she must reference our component from the VS.NET environment by going to Project → Add References and then selecting MathLib.DLL from the directory to which she downloaded it. She then adds the following code to her Console project:

```
Imports MathLib

Module MathProg

Sub Main()
        Dim mClass As MathClass
        Dim result As Integer

        mClass = New MathClass()
        result = mClass.Factorial(5);

End Sub
```

```
End Module
```

Listing 5.9   MathLib client application

Jessica runs her application by pressing F5 and is disheartened to see the following output:

```
Factorial v1.0.0.0
5! = 0
```

Unfortunately, 5! ($5 \times 4 \times 3 \times 2 \times 1$) is 120, not 0. She alerts us to the problem, and consulting our source code we immediately recognize an elementary error that should have been caught. If you look at Listing 5.8, you will see that the nAnswer variable is meant to store the factorial of a given number. Sadly, we forgot to initialize nAnswer, and in lieu of our oversight VB.NET automatically set it to 0. Because the algorithm in Listing 5.8 iteratively multiplies nAnswer to arrive at an answer, clients will always receive a value of 0 for any factorial they compute. This problem is easily solved if we add the following line of code before the program's for loop:

```
nAnswer = 1
```

Updating the Assembly

We promise to produce a new version of the component and e-mail it to Jessica. But how can she be confident that the component she receives is, in fact, from us? Look at Figure 5.5 and you will see that the public key token of our component is f617bdac22953a09. If you use ILDASM.EXE to view the client application's manifest you will see the following:

```
.assembly extern Mathlib
.publickeytoken = (F6 17 BD AC 22 95 3A 09)
```

Jessica's client application references both the assembly name (Mathlib) and the public key token, which can be produced only with our private key. Together, these two entities form a *strong name,* which is guaranteed to be unique. Another company could use the Mathlib namespace, but it could never generate the same public key token. Similarly, Jessica's malicious classmate, Shelina, cannot send her an authentic version of our component because she does not possess our private key. The public key token embedded in the client application assures Jessica that if we don't share our private key, she will always call a component that we produce.

Having updated our source code to reflect the new change, we also modify the AssemblyVersion attribute in our project's `AssemblyInfo.vb` file to reflect the assembly's new version.

```
[assembly:AssemblyVersionAttribute("1.0.0.1")]
```

It is important that we do *not* change the private key used to sign the component. Doing this would give the component a public key token different than v1.0.0.0 of the assembly, and the CLR would have no way of knowing that our new assembly is an update to its predecessor.

Having received the new assembly via e-mail, Jessica installs it as she did before using GACUTIL.EXE. If she examines the GAC's contents, she will see that there are now two versions of the component on her computer (see Figure 5.6).

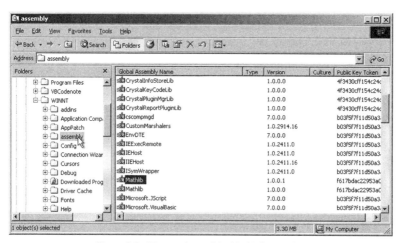

Figure 5.6   Two versions of the MathLib assembly

Jessica's client application does not need to be recompiled in light of the new assembly. The CLR will determine at runtime that v1.0.0.1 is backward compatible with v1.0.0.0 and deliver the latest of the two versions. The client application now correctly outputs:

```
Factorial v1.0.0.1
5! = 120
```

Update with Broken Compatibility

A couple of months down the road, we decide that the Factorial() method is limiting because it returns an integer whose maximum value is roughly 4 billion. This may seem sufficient, but it allows our clients to calculate factorials only up to 12, because 13! > 4 billion. It would be better if it returned a long whose maximum value is considerably larger ($\approx 1.84 \times 10^{19}$). This change breaks compatibility with the old component, however, as the Factorial() method signature is no longer the same. Realizing this, we signify to the CLR that this version of the component is not compatible with its predecessor by giving it an incompatible version number:

```
assembly:AssemblyVersionAttribute("1.5.0.0")]
```

We then update our source to reflect the more capable long variable:

```
Public Class MathClass
    Public Function Factorial (num as integer) as Long
        Dim nAnswer,k As Long

        For k = 1 To num
            nAnswer = nAnswer * k
        Next
        Console.WriteLine("Factorial v1.5.0.0");
        Console.WriteLine("{0}! = {1}",k,nAnswer);

        Return nAnswer
        End Function
End Class
```

Listing 5.10   New version of MathLib

Even if Jessica installs this new version of the component on her computer, the CLR will direct her client to version 1.0.0.1 of the component. Because of the CLR's versioning semantics, new clients can take advantage of the new component, while existing clients continue to rely on the older, compatible one.

If Jessica wanted to take advantage of the new method, she would modify her code (Listing 5.9) by changing the result variable from an integer to a long, then recompile against the new assembly. In order to recompile against the new assembly, Jessica would have to do either one of the following:

1. Select the new assembly as a reference in the VS.NET IDE (and dereference the old assembly in her project)
2. Recompile her project using the /r command-line switch (/r c:\newassembly\MathLib.dll).

Her client application will now reference v1.5.0.0 of the assembly, which will allow her to compute significantly larger factorials.

You may be wondering where, exactly, the various versions of MathSoft.DLL reside on Jessica's machine (where is the GAC?). As of this writing, versions 1.0.0.0, 1.0.0.1, and 1.5.0.0 of the component with the aforementioned public key token can be found in the following directories (they are copied there by GACUTIL.EXE):

```
%Winroot%\assembly\GAC\Mathlib\1.0.0.0__f617bdac22953a09\Mathlib.dll
%Winroot%\assembly\GAC\Mathlib\1.0.0.1__f617bdac22953a09\Mathlib.dll
%Winroot%\assembly\GAC\Mathlib\1.0.0.5__f617bdac22953a09\Mathlib.dll
```

Each version of the component is stored in a directory that is based on its version number and public key token. This is designed to avoid name clashes. If another company released an assembly also called MathLib.DLL, it would reside in a different directory because its public key token would be different. Not surprisingly, the GAC's directories can be modified only by someone with administrator privileges.

Back to Private Assemblies

In light of our knowledge of shared assemblies, we can say a few things about their private cousins. Unlike shared assemblies, private assemblies are not signed with a key and thus do not have strong names. This is permissible because they are to be used by only one application, so unique naming is not a concern. Private assemblies cannot be registered in the GAC using GACUTIL.EXE. Finally, no version checking is performed on private assemblies. Although it is possible to embed a version number into a private assembly using the AssemblyVersion attribute we used in Listing 5.8, it is effectively ignored by the CLR.

VS.NET's Handling of Private Assemblies

In the previous topic we wrote an assembly in C# and then used it from a VS.NET Console application (Listing 5.5). Remember, from the rules we have stated, a private assembly must reside in the directory of the application that uses it. Thus, when you reference a private assembly from VS.NET, it automatically copies it to the project's executable directory. If you look in the Console project's bin directory from the previous topic's example (`\someDiectory\VBCall\bin\`), you will find that it contains the private assembly that you referenced (`MathLib.DLL`).

More than Just Security

Recall that the client application's manifest contained the version and public key token of the MathLib shared assembly. This allows the CLR to load the proper version and ensure that the assembly was authored by us. The public key token also allows the CLR to determine that the assembly's contents (IL code, resources, etc.) have not been corrupted or tampered with. The CLR not only assures Jessica that is she is running our code, it also assures her that the integrity of the assembly has not been compromised since we signed it.

Similarly, if `MathLib.DLL` uses an assembly itself, the CLR would ensure that it runs against the proper version. These integrity checks are performed throughout the chain of callers. Jessica is not only guaranteed that she is calling our code, but that our code is calling the code it expects, and so on, down to the most basic assemblies. You can see that the versioning provided by the .NET Framework is truly rigorous.

HOW AND WHY

Can I Change the Runtime's Versioning Rules?

In some situations it may be desirable to change how the runtime determines the version of a component that is loaded. In our example, we may wish for clients built on v1.0.0.0 of the MathLib component to use v1.5.0.0 if it is available, even though the semantics stipulate that the version numbers are incompatible. This is accomplished by using XML configuration files that override the default versioning behavior of the runtime. An application configuration file can override the versioning rules for the application, and an administrator configuration file can override the policy for the entire machine. Details on using both of these file types can be found at ᴼᴺ»VB050007.

Are Assemblies with Strong Names Trustworthy?

While strong names can assure you that an assembly comes from the same person, they make no guarantees about who that person is. Anyone can generate a private key using SN.EXE and distribute a shared assembly, claiming it originates from company X. Identity is guaranteed only through Microsoft's Authenticode technology (for information, see ᴼᴺ»VB050008).

Do Shared Assemblies Require Version Numbers?

If you do not specify a version number when creating a shared assembly (if we had omitted the `AssemblyVersion` attribute in Listing 3.5), then the compiler will automatically give your component a version number of 0.0.0.0. Clients will be bound to this version number with the normal versioning rules.

Can I Avoid Signing an Assembly until It Is Time to Deploy It?

Quite often, numerous developers work together on a project. It may not be desirable to sign assemblies during the development process, because every developer would need a copy of the private key. Sharing the private key is not only a nuisance, it also increases the chances that the key will be compromised. To address these concerns the .NET Framework exposes the delayed signing option, whereby an assembly is not signed until immediately before it is deployed. Information on delayed signing can be found at ⟨CN⟩VB050009.

Do Assemblies with Strong Names Have to Be Registered in the GAC?

If you give an assembly a strong name by signing it with a private key, you must register it with the GAC only if you want it to be shared. If it is not registered with the GAC, a strong-named assembly will function much like a private one and is accessible only to applications within its directory. These strong private assemblies are, however, more secure than normal private ones, because the CLR will still perform version and signature checking on them.

SUMMARY

Shared assemblies solve the problem of DLL Hell through the Global Assembly Cache (GAC), which allows multiple versions of an assembly to exist side by side on the same machine, and through public key cryptography, which ensures that an assembly can be updated only by an authorized party. To create a shared assembly, you must sign it using a private key, which you generate by using either SN.EXE or VS.NET's Generate Key option.

You must also give the assembly a version number using the CLR's versioning semantics. The version number allows you to specify whether an assembly is backward compatible with its predecessor, allowing the CLR to perform version checking at runtime. The CLR also verifies the integrity of shared assemblies, ensuring that their contents (IL code, resources) have not been compromised since they were created.

Private assemblies don't really solve the DLL Hell problem as much as they avoid it. They are intended to be called by one application and must reside in that application's directory or subdirectory. Because private assemblies don't reside in a prescribed shared area, there is less chance of these assemblies falling prey to malicious (or negligent) installation scripts that wish to update them. Unlike shared assemblies, private ones are not afforded the luxury of version and signature checking. By default, assemblies created in VS.NET are private.

Chapter Summary

Assemblies are the new way components and executables are packaged in the .NET Framework. The EXEs and DLLs created by VB.NET are assemblies. Assemblies contain both IL code and metadata. Metadata describes the types an assembly exposes, the assembly's dependencies, and the assembly's versioning information. The CLR uses an assembly's metadata to ensure that its methods are called in a type-safe manner and that an assembly runs against its proper resources.

Because assemblies are composed of language-neutral IL code, assemblies authored in VB.NET are accessible from languages such as C# and managed C++. Likewise, assemblies authored in other .NET languages can be used easily from VB.NET.

The .NET Framework eradicates the DLL Hell problem through the shared assemblies that reside in the Global Assembly Cache (GAC). A shared assembly must be signed with a private key that allows only authorized parties to update the assembly as it evolves. The GAC is capable of storing multiple versions of the same assembly on one system, and the CLR's versioning rules ensure that clients receive compatible versions of assemblies they expect. The CLR's enforcement of versioning through public key cryptography is considerably stronger than older shared-component models such as Win32 DLLs and COM, where cooperative versioning was dependent on considerate programming practices and voluntary rules.

Chapter 6

—

.NET LANGUAGE FEATURES

In Chapter 4 we saw how two previously unwieldy topics in Visual Basic 6—threading and OOP features such as inheritance—are now intrinsically a part of VB.NET. As we explained in Chapter 4, VB.NET did not really add these features to the language as much as it inherited them from the Common Language Runtime and Base Class Libraries. In this chapter we will examine some of the additional language features in the .NET framework. Like the concepts discussed in Chapter 4, the topics in this chapter are not really VB.NET-specific features as much as they are services provided by the language-neutral CLR.

Chapter 5 introduced the assembly, the new way executable code is packaged in the .NET Framework. The first two topics in this chapter, *attributes* and *reflection,* are centered around assemblies, or more accurately, the metadata contained in an assembly. Attributes are nonprogrammatic statements in your code that insert additional metadata into an assembly. This metadata can then be interpreted by some entity (the CLR, VS.NET, even yourself) to influence some aspect of a VB.NET application (the way it behaves, the manner in which it is deployed, etc.).

Reflection allows a developer to programmatically inspect an assembly's metadata. By reading an assembly's metadata, you can determine (at runtime) the classes it exposes and then invoke the members of those classes. You could, for example, determine that an assembly contained a class called MyClass with method Foo(), then invoke Foo(), all without prior knowledge of the assembly's contents. Reflection can also be used to inspect the metadata that has been embedded by attributes.

In this chapter we will also discuss VB.NET's new event model (WithEvents, RaiseEvent, etc.). We have delayed a discussion of events until this point because they are closely related to another topic in this chapter—*delegates.* Like events, delegates function as callback mechanisms. They can be used to asynchronously notify an interested party that something has occurred (a database has been updated, a client request has been received, etc.). Like VB6's AddressOf operator, a delegate can point to a method or function that is invoked when something interesting occurs. Unlike AddressOf, a delegate can point to a chain of functions, which are successively called when an event is triggered. This capability gives rise to *multicasting,* whereby a single source raises multiple events.

The final topic in this chapter is *garbage collection.* Like the VB6 Runtime, the CLR automatically cleans up after the developer, destroying objects that are no longer being used. The difference is that, unlike the VB6 Runtime, the CLR makes no guarantees regarding when objects are actually destroyed. This unpredictable behavior is referred to as *nondeterministic finalization,* and it has interesting repercussions for the release of resources in VB.NET.

Topic: Attributes

An attribute is a declarative statement in your code that embeds metadata into an assembly to affect its behavior. In the Shared Assemblies topic of the previous chapter, we used an attribute in our Class Library project (Listing 5.8) to specify the assembly's version number:

```
<Assembly: AssemblyVersion("1.0.0.0")>
```

Although this line of code did not programmatically influence our application, it embedded the following metadata into the assembly's manifest (which you can view using ILDASM):

```
.assembly Mathlib
{
  // Other metadata omitted for brevity
  .ver 1:0:0:0
}
```

Listing 6.1   Metadata that results from the AssemblyVersion attribute

When an application uses our assembly, the CLR extracts this section of the metadata to determine whether the versioning requirements of the application have been met. It is important to realize that the CLR is not the only consumer of metadata. Any entity capable of using the reflection technique examined in the next topic can inspect an assembly's metadata and do something useful with it.

As illustrated in the preceding line of code, attributes are enclosed within the < > characters in VB.NET (similarly to a comment being denoted with the ' character). By convention, attribute names end with the word Attribute. Thus, if you look in the MSDN, you will not find an attribute called AssemblyVersion, but rather AssemblyVersionAttribute. We can use the more succinct AssemblyVersion in our code, however, because VB.NET is smart enough to convert it into its longer equivalent.

CONCEPTS

Attribute Example: Using COM+ from the Managed Environment
Attributes are used throughout the .NET Framework as an instrument for application and type configuration. COM+ services, for example, can be accessed via attributes in the System.EnterpriseServices namespace. Recall from Chapter 1 that the CLR uses COM+ to improve component performance in the enterprise application setting. Prior to .NET, using COM+ services required that you manually configure components. Attributes simplify the process considerably.

To take advantage of object pooling, whereby COM+ keeps a pool of objects around in memory to avoid construction and destruction costs, you would use the ObjectPooling attribute:

```
'To access the namespace below, you must add
'System.EnterpriseServices.DLL as a reference
'to your VB.NET project
Imports System.EnterpriseServices

<ObjectPooling(MinPoolSize:=10,MaxPoolSize:=100)> _
Public Class MathClass: Serviced Component
        Public Function Factorial (num As Integer) As Integer
                Dim nAnswer,k As Integer

                For k = 1 To num
                nAnswer = nAnswer * k
                Next
                Console.WriteLine("Factorial v1.0.0.0")
                Console.WriteLine("{0}! = {1}",k,nAnswer)
```

```
                    Return nAnswer
        End Function
End Class
```

Listing 6.2   Using the COM+ ObjectPooling attribute

Listing 6.2 is very similar to Listing 5.8 in the previous chapter. The only difference is that we have used the `ObjectPooling` attribute so that `MathClass` objects are pooled by COM+ once they are created. Note that we have prescribed a minimum pool size of 10 and maximum size of 100 using the `MinPoolSize` and `MaxPoolSize` parameters. The parameters a given attribute accepts can be found in its documentation (the MSDN for attributes found in the Base Class Libraries).

Add the highlighted lines in Listing 6.2 to the VS.NET project we created in Chapter 5 (Listing 5.8). If you build the assembly from within VS.NET and then examine it using ILDASM, you will find the following information in the `MathClass` section of the assembly's metadata:

```
CustomAttribute #1 (0c00000c)
-------------------------------------------------------
CustomAttribute Type: 0a000002
CustomAttributeName:
System.EnterpriseServices.ObjectPoolingAttribute :: instance void
.ctor()
Length: 40
Value : 01 00 02 00 54 08 0b 4d  69 6e 50 6f 6f 6c 53 69
      : 7a 65 02 00 00 00 54 08  0b 4d 61 78 50 6f 6f 6c
      : 53 69 7a 65 05 00 00 00
ctor args: ()
```

Listing 6.3   The metadata that results from the ObjectPooling attribute

Although cryptic, the metadata in Listing 6.3 tells the CLR that when a client uses `MathClass`, the CLR should use the underlying COM+ system to create a pool of 10 objects. By creating objects up front, the cost of subsequently creating them is eliminated. Similarly, when a client has finished using a `MathClass` object, COM+ does not destroy it, but puts it back in the pool to avoid destruction costs.

COM+ Tangent

If you are familiar with COM+, you may recognize that the CLR must do a lot of work to enable object pooling. Among other things, the CLR must dynamically create a COM+ application, configure an underlying component to support object pooling (with our specified parameters), and serve as a buffer between the unmanaged (COM+) and managed (VB.NET) worlds. Luckily, all of these operations are transparently performed for us when we use the `ObjectPooling` attribute. If you have used COM+ in a traditional capacity, you can see that the .NET Framework greatly simplifies COM+ integration via attributes. If you look in the `System.EnterpriseServices` namespace, you will find additional attributes that allow you to take advantage of COM+ services such as just-in-time activation, queued components, and transactions. Details on COM+ services can be found at ⊶CN⟩VB060001.

There are a couple of caveats to keep in mind when using COM+ services from the .NET Framework:

1. The assembly can be deployed only on a COM+-enabled operating system (Windows 2000, Windows XP). Thus our modified assembly in Listing 6.3 will no longer run on Windows 98 and Windows NT, even though these systems are supported by the CLR.
2. The assembly must have a strong name. That is, as discussed in the Shared Assemblies topic in Chapter 5, it must be signed with a globally unique private key, as was the case in our Class Library project in Listing 5.3. This stipulation can be understood only in light of low-level COM+ details, but basically ensures that the underlying COM+ application that is created is given a unique name.

Back to Attributes

The two attributes we have illustrated (`AttributeVersion` and `ObjectPooling`) highlight the basic premise of attributes in the .NET Framework:

> Attributes embed additional metadata into an assembly, which is used in some fashion to influence application behavior.

Both attributes we have examined exhibit this characteristic. At the beginning of this chapter, we saw that `AttributeVersion` resulted in the metadata in Listing 6.1, which the CLR used for version control. The metadata in Listing 6.3, courtesy of the `ObjectPooling` attribute, instructed the CLR to use the COM+ infrastructure to pool `MathClass` objects.

You will see attributes employed throughout the .NET Framework. The `Conditional` attribute, for example, can be used in place of VB6's

#Const, #If, and #End IF conditional compilation directives. The Serializable attribute is used to specify whether an object can be transferred to a remote location—an important capability for .NET's remoting technology that we discuss in Chapter 9. Information on both of these attributes can be found at ⌐CN⌐VB060002.

Custom Attributes

In addition to the predefined attributes that come packaged with the .NET Framework (such as AttributeVersion and ObjectPooling), you can also author your own custom attributes in VB.NET. By writing a custom attribute, *you* determine the metadata that is inserted into an assembly when the attribute is applied on a given type (a class, a method, etc.). Similarly, when the type is instantiated, the CLR extracts your metadata, which you can then use in some meaningful manner.

We will not delve into the details of authoring custom attributes here. Those interested may consult ⌐CN⌐VB060003 for details and examples. In practice, you are much more likely to *utilize* attributes in the .NET Framework instead of writing your own. Note that custom attributes written in VB.NET can also be used in C# and managed C++, thanks to the language neutrality of the CLR.

SUMMARY

Attributes are nonprogrammatic statements in VB.NET code that embed metadata into an assembly, where it can be retrieved and used in a meaningful manner. There are two types of attributes in the .NET Framework: predefined and custom. *Predefined attributes* are accessed through the Base Class Libraries, and the metadata they produce is used by some Microsoft entity (such as the CLR or Windows Form Designer) to influence application behavior. *Custom attributes* allow developers to place their own metadata into assemblies, the contents and purpose of which are entirely up to the attribute's author.

By convention, attribute names end with Attribute (e.g., ObjectPoolingAttribute). VB.NET provides a syntactical shortcut by automatically appending this suffix to attributes. In VB.NET, therefore, you can write ObjectPooling instead of the more verbose ObjectPoolingAttribute.

Topic: Reflection

Reflection is a technique used to programmatically inspect an assembly's metadata. As we learned in Chapter 5, metadata describes all the types an assembly exposes. You can thus use reflection to determine the classes an assembly contains, the members exposed by the classes, and the parameters the members expect, all without prior knowledge of the assembly. Using this information, you can call a class's method dynamically. In the previous topic we learned that another source of metadata is attributes. Not surprisingly, reflection can also determine which attributes are applied to a given type.

CONCEPTS

Type Hierarchy

To understand reflection, you must understand the hierarchy of types in the .NET Framework. The foundation of this hierarchy is the Common Type System that we saw in Chapter 1. Using the CTS, you can build more complex types such as methods, properties, and events (events are described in the next topic). Methods and properties are encapsulated within a class, itself contained within an assembly (or possibly a module). The ladder of types in the .NET Framework is illustrated in Figure 6.1.

```
AppDomains:
   Assemblies:
      Modules:
         Class:
              Fields
              Properties
              Events
              Methods
                  CTS
```

Figure 6.1   .NET type hierarchy

The classes found in the System.Reflection namespace allow you to traverse up and down the ladder of .NET types. Using reflection, therefore, you could determine the types an assembly exposes (its classes, structures, etc.). Similarly, given a class, you could determine the types it contains (the class's methods and member variables), as well as their constituent types (method parameters and return values). In the upcoming example, we will see how one can dynamically load an assembly and call a method in one of its classes.

AppDomains

At the top of the type ladder in Figure 6.1 is an entity called an App-Domain. You can think of an AppDomain as the conceptual equivalent of a running application or process. When you run an .EXE produced by Visual Basic 6, Windows constructs a dedicated process for your program. Because your application is in its own process, it is protected from other applications that might misbehave. Similarly, when you run an application produced by VB.NET, the CLR houses it in an AppDomain. Just as a process separates applications in the unmanaged realm, an AppDomain serves as the protective boundary for programs executing in the .NET Framework.

VB6 developers may be familiar with the term *in-process*. When you use an ActiveX control or component from your VB6 application, it is usually brought into your application's process (hence the term *in-process*). Similarly, when you use an assembly from a VB.NET program, it is brought into the AppDomain of your application. An AppDomain, therefore, *contains* assemblies—hence its placement at the top of the .NET type system.

AppDomains and Windows Architecture

You may wonder about the relationship between an AppDomain and a bona fide Windows process. After all, the CLR runs on top of Windows, so the two must be somehow related. As previously established, Windows processes isolate applications from one another. Because processes herald from the days prior to .NET, they must provide robust protection against native code, making them expensive to create and tear down. Because IL code operates inside the CLR, it can be afforded the same protection without the costly construction of a process. The .NET Framework saves resources by allowing multiple AppDomains to exist in one process. If the CLR must shut down an AppDomain, it can do so without disrupting other AppDomains in the same process. It is proper, therefore, to think of an AppDomain as a lightweight process, made possible due to the increased protection provided by the CLR.

If a Windows process can contain multiple AppDomains, you may wonder why it is not at the top of Figure 6.1. Its exclusion from the .NET type system is because a process is largely a Windows architecture concept, not a .NET concept. The relationship between an AppDomain and a process is simply part of the architectural design of the CLR—it has no bearing on how your VB.NET applications operate. When writing programs in VB.NET, let the CLR worry about processes; your applications execute within AppDomains.

EXAMPLE

Basic Reflection
The merits of reflection are best illustrated by example. Consider the straightforward code in Listing 6.4.

```
Public Class MathClass
    Public SomeVar As String
    Public Function Add(a As Integer, b As Integer) As Integer
        Return a + b
    End Function
End Class
```

Listing 6.4   MathClass Library

Add this code to a Console Library project called MathLib and build it from the VS.NET IDE. From our discussion in Chapter 5, we learned that the resulting `MathLib.dll` file contains metadata that describes the assembly's types. As Chapter 5 also demonstrated, we can use a utility called ILDASM to inspect the assembly's metadata. You can also examine an assembly's metadata programmatically at runtime using reflection, as demonstrated in Listing 6.5.

```
Imports System.Reflection
Imports MathLib 'needed to call MathClass

Module Module1
    Sub Main()
        Dim mC As MathClass
        Dim Members As MemberInfo()
        Dim mi As MemberInfo
        Dim T As Type

        mC = New MathClass()
        T = mC.GetType()

        'Get all the members in the MathClass type and
        'Print them out
```

```
    Members = T.GetMembers(BindingFlags.Default)

    For Each mi In Members
        Console.WriteLine(" {0} = {1}", mi.MemberType,
            mi.ToString())
    Next
    End Sub
End Module
```

Listing 6.5   Using reflection to inspect MathClass

Copy the code in Listing 6.5 into a Console Application project and reference the `MathLib.dll` assembly using VS.NET's Add Reference option. Run the application by pressing F5 and you will see the following output:

```
Field = System.String SomeVar
Method = Int32 GetHashCode()
Method = Boolean Equals(System.Object)
Method = System.String ToString()
Method = Int32 Add(Int32, Int32)
Method = System.Type GetType()
Constructor = Void .ctor()
```

Listing 6.6   Reflection output

As the output in Listing 6.6 illustrates, we can use reflection to determine the types exposed by the `MathClass` class. Interestingly, we seem to have picked up more members in the class than it originally contained (see Listing 6.4). Remember that all types in the .NET Framework inherit from `System.Object`. Thus, in addition to our two members (`SomeVar()` and `Add()`), `MathClass` also inherits the members of `System.Object` (`Equals()`, `ToString()`, etc.).

The reflection process is quite simple if we break it down line by line. An object's metadata is accessed through its `Type` class, which is retrieved using its `GetType()` method. As depicted in Listing 6.6, `GetType()` is implemented by `System.Object`, so it can be called on any object:

```
T = mC.GetType()
```

`MathClass`'s type information can now be accessed through the `Type` class just obtained. One of the members of the `Type` class is `GetMembers()`, which returns `MathClass`'s members:

```
Members = T.GetMembers(BindingFlags.Default)
```

GetMembers() accepts one parameter, which determines the members it should return. In the preceding code, we asked for the basic class members using the BindingFlags enumeration found in the System.Reflection namespace. You can vary those members returned by GetMembers() using the elements found in this enumeration. To obtain private members, for example, you would use the BindingFlags.NonPublic element. After obtaining the class's members, Listing 6.5 iterates through the MemberInfo array and outputs the type information in Listing 6.6.

As can be seen from this example, reflection is a straightforward process. If there is metadata in an assembly, you can most certainly retrieve it using the System.Reflection classes; it is just a matter of finding the appropriate class to use. To this end, the next example illustrates how we would use reflection to inspect the metadata embedded by an attribute.

Reflection Attribute Example
As illustrated in the previous topic, attributes also insert metadata into an assembly. Recall that the ObjectPooling attribute in Listing 6.2 manifested itself as the metadata in Listing 6.3. Not surprisingly, we can use reflection to inspect attribute metadata as well. To illustrate this technique, insert the following highlighted lines into the MathLib project you created in Listing 6.5.

```
Imports System.EnterpriseServices

<ObjectPoolingAttribute(MinPoolSize:=10, MaxPoolSize:=100)> _
Public Class MathClass
    Public SomeVar As String
    Public Function Add(ByVal a As Integer, ByVal b As Integer) _
        As Integer
      Return a + b
    End Function
End Class
```

Listing 6.7   The ObjectPooling attribute

Recompile the MathLib project (don't forget to reference System.EnterpriseServices.dll) and reload the Console Application project you created. Add the following line to the top of Listing 6.6:

```
Imports System.EnterpriseServices
```

As with the MathLib project, you will need to reference System.EnterpriseServices.dll. Now add the following code to Listing 6.6 (after the end of the For loop).

```
Dim attributes As Attribute()
Dim attrib As Attribute
attributes = System.Attribute.GetCustomAttributes(T)

Console.WriteLine("Custom attributes used on this type: {0}",
  attributes.Length)

For Each attrib In attributes
   Console.WriteLine(attrib)
   If TypeOf attrib Is ObjectPoolingAttribute Then
      Dim o As ObjectPoolingAttribute
      o = CType(attrib, ObjectPoolingAttribute)
      Console.WriteLine("MinPoolSize: {0}, MaxPoolSize: {1}",
         o.MinPoolSize, o.MaxPoolSize)
   End If
Next
```

Listing 6.8   Using reflection to retrieve attribute metadata

To determine whether any attributes were applied to MathClass, Listing 6.8 uses the System.Attribute class's GetCustomAttributes() method. It prints out any attributes that were applied to MathClass, and, if the attribute happens to be an ObjectPoolingAttribute, it also prints out the minimum and maximum size of the object pool. It may seem confusing that GetCustomAttributes() detected a *predefined* attribute. (From the function name, you would imagine it would retrieve only user-created attributes.) The confusion quickly dissipates if we realize the following:

- All attributes *are* custom attributes. The only difference is that predefined ones have already been written and packaged by Microsoft in the BCL.

Thus, GetCustomAttributes() will pick up all of the attributes applied on a given type. If you run the modified application, you will see the following output (in addition to the output in Listing 6.7):

```
Custom attributes used on this type: 1
System.EnterpriseServices.ObjectPoolingAttribute
MinPoolSize: 10, MaxPoolSize: 100
```

This listing shows that our reflection program correctly determines that we applied the `ObjectPoolingAttribute` to `MathClass`. It also reports a pool size of 10 to 100, which is in agreement with the attribute parameters we applied in Listing 6.8.

Reflection to Invoke Members

The reflection techniques examined thus far may not seem particularly useful. Although we have inspected an assembly's metadata, we haven't really done anything with it. The true versatility of reflection becomes apparent when you realize that you can use it to invoke methods at runtime without prior knowledge of the types that contain them. Before we illustrate this useful technique, let us consider how dynamic invocation worked under VB6.

VB6's Object Type

If you have used ActiveX components or VB classes in Visual Basic 6, you may be familiar with the concepts of compile-time and runtime checking. Consider the `MathClass` class we wrote in Listing 6.5. If we were to use this class and employ compile-time checking in VB6, our code would look something like this:

```
dim mc as New MathClass
mc.Foo()
```

Because we dimensioned `mc` explicitly as a `MathClass`, VB6 can correctly determine that `Foo()` is not a supported member of `mc`. Thus, it can determine at compile-time that we have a problem. If you are familiar with ActiveX or COM, you will notice that compile-time checking is analogous with the term *early binding*.

If we were to employ runtime checking in our program we would use VB6's Object type, and our code would look something like this:

```
dim mc as Object
Set mc = new MathClass()
mc.Foo()
```

Because we have dimensioned mc as a generic Object, VB6 will compile and run the application. It will not perform type checking until runtime, at which point it will determine that Foo() cannot be invoked. Thus you will not get an error when you compile the application, but you will get one when you run the application. Runtime checking is equivalent to *late binding* in COM and ActiveX.

Why would you ever want to use the Object type, considering that our compile-time example is more robust? As always, there is a trade-off. Although the Object type doesn't allow for compile-time checking, it can be useful when you don't have prior knowledge of the type you will be calling. The Object type is a shot in the dark. If the underlying object supports Foo(), then all is well; if it doesn't, then a runtime error occurs. The primary shortcoming of VB6's Object type is that you cannot determine whether Foo() is a valid method at runtime. That is, you cannot avoid runtime errors by writing something like this:

```
if mc supports method Foo()
    mc.Foo()
```

Listing 6.9   Runtime/late binding in VB6

As you might guess, reflection can be used to determine a type's members at runtime. This capability, combined with the reflection invocation classes we will examine in the upcoming example, provides a solution to the problem of invoking dynamically discovered methods.

Reflection Invocation Example

In this example we will call the MathClass.Add() method from Listing 6.5. Most important, we will do this without prior knowledge of the class—we will not include it as a reference in our VS.NET project.

To invoke Add() without referencing the MathClass assembly, we need a way of loading MathLib.dll at runtime. This is accomplished using the LoadFrom() method of the System.Assembly class. Once the assembly is loaded, we traverse down the .NET type ladder (shown in Figure 6.1) to find Add(). If we find a method called Add(), we then check to see whether it accepts the parameters we expect. If it passes this test, we finally invoke the method using a special class called Activator, also found in the System namespace. Listing 6.10 gives the full source code.

```
'Put this code in a Console Application's Main() method

Dim methods As MethodInfo()
Dim method As MethodInfo
```

```
Dim types As Type()
Dim type As Type

'Dynamically load the assembly:
Dim asm As Reflection.Assembly
asm = Reflection.Assembly.LoadFrom("\SomeDir\MathLib.dll")

'Determine the types (classes) it contains:
types = asm.GetTypes()
For Each type In types

  Console.WriteLine("Searching Class: {0} for an Add() method", _
    type)
  methods = type.GetMethods(BindingFlags.Default)

  For Each method In methods
     If method.Name = "Add" Then
      Dim pInfo As ParameterInfo()
      pInfo = method.GetParameters
      ' Does Add()take 2 parameters, both of which are int32s?
      If pInfo.Length = 2 Then
        If pInfo(0).ParameterType.ToString() = "System.Int32" _
            And (pInfo(1).ParameterType.ToString() = _
            "System.Int32" Then
          Console.WriteLine(_
            "Add() found with two Int32 parameters.")
          Dim o, returnvalue As Object
          Dim param(1) As Object
          o = Activator.CreateInstance(type)
          param(0) = 1: param(1) = 2
          returnvalue = method.Invoke(o, param)
           Console.WriteLine(_
            "Dynamically Invoked Add(1,2) = {0}",_
            returnvalue)
            End If
          End If
        End If
    Next
 Next
```

Listing 6.10   Dynamic invocation using reflection

The first bolded line in Listing 6.10 loads the MathClass assembly at runtime (change this line to reflect wherever MathLib.dll is located on your machine). After loading the assembly, we traverse through all of its types, looking for an Add() method that accepts two integer variables. When such a method is found, it is called using the Invoke() method of the MethodInfo class:

```
Dim param(1) As Object
o = Activator.CreateInstance(type)
param(0) = 1: param(1) = 2
returnvalue = method.Invoke(o, param)
```

As the preceding code illustrates, parameters are passed to the Invoke()method as an array of objects, with the first element corresponding to the first parameter and so on. It is up to us to ensure that we deliver an object array whose size and contents match the parameters and types that the method expects. If we fail to do this, the CLR will throw a TargetParameter or Argument exception. If you run the application in Listing 6.11 (by creating a Console application in VS.NET), it will produce the following output:

```
Searching Class: MathLib.MathClass for an Add() method
Add() found with two Int32 parameters.
Dynamically Invoked Add(1,2) = 3
```

The power of Listing 6.10 is its ability to execute MathClass's Add() method without a priori (beforehand) knowledge of the class. And, unlike VB6's late-binding Object mechanism in Listing 6.9, if the underlying class does not contain an Add() method, we will not receive a runtime error. Instead, Listing 6.10 will simply determine that there is no valid method to be called and will gracefully terminate. This added capability is not a feature of VB.NET, but a by-product of the self-describing nature of assemblies.

Note that Listing 6.10 will work with *any* assembly in the .NET Framework. As long as the assembly contains a class with a method called Add (which accepts two integer parameters), Listing 6.10 will invoke it. Of course, there is no guarantee about what another assembly's Add() might do. It could subtract two numbers, format your hard drive, and so forth.

Reflection "Emit"
Just as reflection can be used to retrieve and interpret metadata, it can be used to construct and emit it. The classes found in the

System.Reflection.Emit namespace allow metadata for new types to be generated in memory and used at runtime. In fact, you can dynamically create an entire assembly, its classes and methods, and the IL code behind them. The in-memory assembly can then be used by other applications. Examples of this versatile procedure can be found at ^{CN}VB060004.

HOW AND WHY

How Do I Prevent Reflection from Calling the Private Methods of My Class?

In Listing 6.10 we used the BindingFlags.Default parameter to detect the members of our class. Had we used BindingFlags.NonPublic, we could have invoked private methods of the class. This is a powerful technique, but a concern for developers who don't want their private methods being called.

Whether or not reflection can call private methods depends on the security policy where the code originates (locally, the Internet, etc.). Code that originates from the local hard drive is automatically given the right to detect and invoke the private methods of a class. You can alter this behavior by changing the security policy for the entire machine using a utility called CASPOL.EXE. Details on how to do this can be found at ^{CN}VB060011.

SUMMARY

Reflection allows you to programmatically traverse through an assembly's metadata. Using the classes found in the System.Reflection namespace, you can inspect either standard type-describing metadata produced by an IL compiler (VB.NET, C#, etc.) or metadata produced by an attribute.

In addition to being able to ascertain type information at runtime, reflection allows you to invoke the members of the very types you are inspecting. This capability is superior to Visual Basic 6's late-binding mechanisms, whereby you could call a class in a late-bound fashion but couldn't ensure that runtime errors wouldn't result.

Topic: Events and Delegates

In this topic we look at two closely related features in VB.NET: events and delegates. Both of these features facilitate *asynchronous notification*—the ability of some entity (an object, a function) to inform a client that something has occurred without requiring the client to explicitly wait for the notification. The premise behind asynchronous notification is increased efficiency. Because a program does not have to wait idly for an object or function to respond, it is free to perform other operations.

Asynchronous notification is ubiquitous in Visual Basic. It is so commonplace, in fact, that it easy to forget you are employing it. Consider the VB6 code in Listing 6.11, which responds to the click of a button:

```
Private Sub Command1_Click()
    MsgBox "Hello World!"
End Sub
```

Listing 6.11   VB6 event code

Command1_Click is an event handler, because it *handles* the event raised by the VB Runtime when the button is clicked. Even if your program is doing other things, such as sorting an array of numbers or writing to a file, a message box will be displayed when the button is pressed. In this way, the VB Runtime is asynchronously notifying the client (you) of an event (the button click).

Starting with VB5, developers could write classes that exposed their own events. If you wrote a database class, for example, you might expose an event called UpdateComplete(), which notifies clients that underlying data operations have finished.

In this topic we will look at VB.NET's new event structure. Because the Base Class Libraries (BCL) utilize VB.NET's new event mechanisms, you will come across them in even the simplest VB.NET programs. The VB6 code in Listing 6.11, for example, is entirely different in VB.NET.

Delegates, the second subject in the section, are closely related to another VB5 novelty: the AddressOf operator. As its name suggests, AddressOf is used to provide the address of a VB function. AddressOf was a significant appendage to the language because it gave developers the ability to leverage Windows API functions that used *callbacks* (the Assemblies and Metadata topic in Chapter 5 explains how to call the Windows API from VB6). By giving a Windows API function the address of a VB function, Windows can *call back* the VB function when something important occurs (e.g., when a file is copied).

Delegates replace callback functions in the .NET Framework. Delegates are significant because they can point to numerous functions, all of which are called when the delegate is invoked. As we will see, this powerful capability allows for *multicasting,* which is when one source notifies numerous parties of an event.

CONCEPTS

VB.NET Events

Writing a class that exposes events in VB.NET is virtually equivalent to doing the same in VB6. You use the event keyword to declare the event, then use the RaiseEvent keyword to trigger it. Listing 6.13 illustrates a class called StockInfo that exposes an event called PriceChanged.

```
Class StockInfo

    Public Event PriceChanged(price As Double)
    Public Sub Start()
        'For simplicity, just raise the event once, although
        'in reality we would loop continually and raise the event
        'whenever the stock price changed.
        RaiseEvent PriceChanged(100.00)
    End Sub
End Class
```

Listing 6.12   A VB.NET class that exposes an event

As in VB6, clients would write an event handler to be notified when StockInfo raised the PriceChanged event. Remember, the idea behind events is efficiency: by subscribing to the event, the client is free to do other things until the event is raised. Subscribing to an event in VB.NET is a little different than VB6. You still declare a class using the WithEvents keyword:

```
Dim WithEvents stck As StockInfo
```

What has changed, however, is the name of the associated event handler. In VB6, event handlers adhere to the ObjectName_EventName naming convention. In Listing 6.12, for example, the button's event handler is named Command1_Click. Similarly, a VB6 event handler of the StockInfo class would be called something like Stck_PriceChanged. In VB.NET, you can call an event handler whatever you like, but you must associate it with the class's event using a new keyword called Handles:

```
Private Sub MyEvent(price As Double) Handles stck.PriceChanged
    Console.WriteLine("Stock Price Changed!")
End Sub
```

Listing 6.13   Subscribing to an event in VB.NET

This is why, way back in Chapter 1, Listing 1.3, VS.NET automatically used the Handles keyword when we wanted to write code that responded to the click of a button:

```
Private Sub Button1_Click(ByVal sender As System.Object, _
  ByVal e As System.EventArgs) Handles Button1.Click
    MessageBox.Show("Hello World")
End Sub
```

We delve into the details of Windows Forms event handlers in Chapter 7, but the preceding code basically associates the Button1_Click procedure with Button1's click event. As we intended, whenever Button1's click event is raised (when someone presses the button), Button1_Click will be invoked and the message box will be displayed.

Multiple Event Handlers

VB.NET has an additional capability—you can write multiple event handlers for a single event. Thus, in addition to the code in Listing 6.7, we could associate a second event handler with the PriceChanged event:

```
Private Sub MyEvent2(price As Double) Handles stck.PriceChanged
    'Do something with the Stock Price
End Sub
```

As a result of this association, both MyEvent and MyEvent2 will be invoked whenever the PriceChanged event is raised, something that cannot be done in Visual Basic 6. The order in which the functions are invoked depends on the order in which they establish their association to the event. Because MyEvent appears first in code, it will execute before MyEvent2. We revisit event handlers when we examine the Windows Forms classes in Chapter 7.

Delegates

Delegates are best understood against VB6's AddressOf operator. Recall that this operator is used to obtain the memory address of a VB procedure (or function) and is often used when calling the Windows API. By giving an API function the address of a VB procedure, it can call you back to notify you of some event.

An example of such a function is CopyFileEx(), which can be used to copy a file. One of the parameters of CopyFileEx() is the address of function that it calls after a certain number of bytes have been copied. For example, if you were copying a file that was 100,000 bytes long, CopyFileEx()could call back your function after every 10,000 bytes were copied. This type of notification mechanism would allow you to display some type of operation status to the user (such as a progress bar). We will not reproduce the code here, but the interested reader is directed to ᵒ⤳VB060005 for a VB6 CopyFileEx() example.

The Shortcomings of AddressOf

Although the AddressOf operator can be used to specify the address of a function, it does not guarantee the parameters the function accepts. This limitation is problematic, because there is no way to ensure that the callback function is type-safe. For example, the function that CopyFileEx() expects must accept the following parameters:

```
Public Function CopyProgressCallback ( _
  ByVal TotalFileSize As Currency, _
  ByVal TotalBytesTransferred As Currency, _
  ByVal StreamSize As Currency, _
  ByVal StreamBytesTransferred As Currency, _
  ByVal dwStreamNumber As Long, _
  ByVal dwCallbackReason As Long, _
  ByVal hSourceFile As Long, _
  ByVal hDestinationFile As Long, _
  lpData As Long) As Long
```

Lisitng 6.14   Callback function expected by CopyFileEx()

Because AddressOf has no concept of function parameters, we can just as easily provide CopyFileEx() with the following, unsuitable, function:

```
Public Function UhOh(ByVal problem As Long) as Long
```

The results of this incompatible assignment are disastrous. When CopyFileEx()attempts to call our function, it will think it is calling a function whose signature matches the one depicted in Listing 6.14. Because it is calling the UhOh function, whose parameters are considerably different, an unrecoverable application error will occur and the program will shut down. Even worse, there is no way for Visual Basic 6 to catch this error at compile time or runtime, given the ambiguous nature of AddressOf.

Enter Delegates

Delegates solve the aforementioned problems of AddressOf, and they also offer a number of useful innovations:

1. Delegates are type-safe. They specify the parameters a callback function must accept to avoid the precarious situation highlighted in Listing 6.14.
2. In addition to global functions, delegates can point to the class methods. (In VB6, AddressOf could point only to global functions.)
3. Delegates can wrap a chain of functions. When the delegate is invoked, each function in the chain is called.

The second point may puzzle some readers. What happens if a delegate is wrapping a class's method and the class is removed from memory? Invoking the delegate is now dangerous, since it no longer points to a valid location. Remember, however, that because both the class and delegate are running within the CLR, such a situation will never occur—the class will never be garbage-collected if a delegate is wrapping one of its methods.

EXAMPLE

We illustrate delegates through a class called AlarmClock, which wakes up a client application after a given amount of time. To wake up client applications (to call them back when it is time), AlarmClock must first define a delegate that clients use to request wake-up calls:

```
Public Delegate Sub WakeMeUp(ByVal message As String)
```

This definition prescribes that clients must provide AlarmClock with a delegate accepting a string parameter if they wish to be called back. Once AlarmClock wakes the application up by invoking the delegate, the client can do whatever it wants with the string (print it on the screen, write it to a file etc.). To request a wake-up call, AlarmClock exposes a method called RequestWakeup:

```
Public Sub RequestWakeup(ByVal wakeupFunc As WakeMeUp, _
  ByVal SecondsTillWakeup As Integer)
```

The first argument of this method is the delegate we previously defined. The second parameter is the amount of seconds AlarmClock waits before calling back the client application. The full AlarmClock source is given in Listing 6.15.

```
Public Class AlarmClock

Public Delegate Sub WakeMeUp(ByVal message As String)

Public Sub RequestWakeup(ByVal wakeupFunc As WakeMeUp, _
  ByVal SecondsTillWake As Integer)

    'Wait for the specified period of time, before waking up
    'Use the DateTime class in the System namespace to delay:
    Dim delayTime As Integer
    Dim tBefore As Long
    Dim dt As DateTime
    dt = New DateTime()

    ' Delay for the specified time:
    dt = DateTime.Now
    tBefore = dt.Ticks
    Do While (dt.Ticks - tBefore < SecondsTillWake *
        System.TimeSpan.TicksPerSecond)
        dt = DateTime.Now
    Loop

    ' Time has expired, so wake the client up by
    ' calling the delegate:
    wakeupFunc("Time to get up!")
  End Sub

End Class
```

Listing 6.15   The AlarmClock class

As shown in Listing 6.15, RequestWakeup call delays for the specified period of time before waking up the client application by invoking the provided delegate. Copy Listing 6.15 into a Console project in VS.NET. Then insert the following client code into your project, which uses the AlarmClock class.

```
Module Module1

    'The funciton we will be called back on:
    Sub MyWakeupFunction(ByVal message As String)
        Console.WriteLine( _
        "I was woken up. AlarmClock said: {0}", message)
    End Sub

    Sub Main()
      Dim aC As AlarmClock
      aC = New AlarmClock() 'Remember, no Set!

      'Construct the delegate:
      Dim wakeup As AlarmClock.WakeMeUp
      wakeup = New AlarmClock.WakeMeUp(AddressOf MyWakeupFunction)

      Console.WriteLine("Requesting WakeupCall")
      'Tell AlarmClock to call us back in 3 seconds:
      aC.RequestWakeup(wakeup, 3)

      'Wait for user to press a key before exiting application
      Console.Read()
    End Sub
End Module
```

Listing 6.16   AlarmClock client application

As the highlighted code in Listing 6.16 illustrates, a delegate must be constructed before we can request a wake-up call from AlarmClock. Unlike AlarmClock, which *accepts* a delegate, the client application that *provides* one does not use the delegate keyword. Instead, it first declares a function whose signature matches that of delegate:

```
Sub MyWakeupFunction(ByVal message As String)
```

Then the client application creates a delegate that wraps the function. In VB.NET, you create a delegate as you would a class, via the New keyword. When declaring a delegate, you pass it the address of the function it will wrap. Note that function addresses are still resolved with the AddressOf operator:

```
wakeup = New AlarmClock.WakeMeUp(AddressOf MyWakeupFunction)
```

By employing this roundabout process, VB.NET can ensure the function wrapped by the delegate accepts the same parameters as the delegate itself. If you were to modify MyWakeupFunction() so that it accepted an integer instead of a string, VB.NET would inform you of the following:

```
Module1.vb(42): Could not find method 'Public Sub MyWakeupFunction(message
As Integer)' with the same signature as the delegate 'Delegate Sub
WakeMeUp(message As String)'.
```

Such compile-time safety checking is in contrast to the problematic situation in Listing 6.15, where VB6 could not ensure that the callback function accepted the right number of parameters. As you can see, the type-safe nature of delegates leads to a more robust notification scheme.

Copy Listing 6.16 into your Console Application, run it by pressing F5, and you will see the following output:

```
Requesting WakeupCall
I was woken up. AlarmClock said: Time to get up!
```

Three seconds after the first line of the output, the client application will be woken up by the AlarmClock class and display the second line.

Delegate Chains

One of the most useful features of delegates is their ability to wrap a chain of functions, all of which are called when the delegate is invoked. To create a delegate chain, you must use the Combine() method of the System.Delegate class. If you provide this method with two delegates, it will produce a third delegate that chains them together. Thus, by adding the following function to Listing 6.17:

```
Sub MyWakeupFunction2(ByVal message As String)
    Console.WriteLine( _
       "I was ALSO woken up. AlarmClock said: {0}",
       message)
End Sub
```

you can create a delegate chain with the following line of code (add it after the bolded code in Listing 6.17):

```
wakeup = System.Delegate.Combine(wakeup, New _
         AlarmClock.WakeMeUp(AddressOf MyWakeupFunction2))
```

If you are wondering why we constructed the chain using `System.Delegate.Combine()` instead of `Delegate.Combine()`, it is because the latter statement creates a syntactical dilemma for the VB.NET compiler due to the `Delegate` keyword designation in the language; VB.NET can't handle having "Delegate" as both a system-level class instance and a keyword used for creating new classes. Run the application and you will see that both functions are called back when the application is woken up:

```
Requesting WakeupCall
I was woken up. AlarmClock said: Time to get up!
I was ALSO woken up. AlarmClock said: Time to get up!
```

Thus, one entity (`AlarmClock`) has invoked two functions (`MyWakeupFunction` and `MyWakeupFunction2`), which is commonly known as *multicasting*. Delegates can also invoke functions across App-Domains, meaning that one application can call back another one.

Keep in mind that the `AlarmClock` class has no idea it is calling a chain of functions. It simply invokes the delegate, which determines that a chain of functions is being wrapped and calls them accordingly. A delegate must do a lot of underlying work to facilitate this behavior. This may seem confusing given that a delegate is nothing more than a keyword in VB.NET. Delegates are very simple to use up front, but there is a lot of work going on underneath the hood.

When you use a delegate in VB.NET, it is actually employing a special class behind the scenes called `System.MulticastDelegate`. This class takes care of intricate details of invoking function chains, ensuring callback-function type safety, and so on. Unless you want to deal with delegates on a nuts-and-bolts level, simply use delegates as we have illustrated and let VB.NET handle the rest. Those with a penchant for details can visit ⟋ᴺ VB060006 for information on the internal use of `System.MulticastDelegate`.

What about Asynchronous Behavior?

At the beginning of this chapter we claimed that, like events, delegates facilitate asynchronous notification. Unfortunately, our `AlarmClock` class in Listing 6.16 doesn't appear to live up to this assertion. After `AlarmClock` receives a wake-up request, it doesn't immediately return to the client, but waits for the prescribed amount of time before calling the client back. In other words, the main virtue of asynchronous notification—the ability of a client to continue operating after a request has been made—is absent from our implementation.

To provide truly asynchronous behavior, the `RequestWakeup()` method in Listing 6.16 should return immediately to the client and then invoke the delegate at some point after that. This is a more involved procedure that requires using the threading classes we saw in Chapter 4. For the sake of brevity, we have omitted this more complex approach. However, a truly asynchronous `AlarmClock` class can be found at ⌀VB060007.

The Relationship between Delegates and Events

Delegates and events are remarkably similar. Both can be used in asynchronous notification situations. Both facilitate multicasting; the earlier discussion on multiple event handlers illustrated that you can associate numerous event handlers with a single event, and delegates afford the same functionality through chaining.

As you may have guessed, the relationship between delegates and events is more than just a coincidental overlap in functionality— delegates *are* the underlying architecture behind events in VB.NET. When you use the `event`, `RaiseEvents`, and `WithEvents` keywords in VB.NET, the compiler translates your event statements into delegate equivalents.

If you are developing solely in VB.NET, you can use events as we have illustrated and let the VB.NET compiler take care of the details. If you wish to write events in C# or managed C++, however, you are not afforded such abstraction and must understand the relationship between events and delegates in the .NET Framework. We illustrate this relationship at ⌀VB060008. Those of you familiar with the underpinnings of previous versions of Visual Basic will note that delegates mark the end of COM's ConnectionPoint model that drove events in Visual Basic 6.

Even though VB.NET masks the relationship between events and delegates, an understanding of delegates is still important, as many BCL classes utilize them directly. And, as we discuss in Chapter 8, if your VB.NET program utilizes Windows API functions with callbacks, it must also use delegates.

HOW AND WHY

Can I Remove Functions from Delegate Chains?

Just as you can add a function to a delegate chain using the `Combine()`

method, you can remove one using the `Remove()` method. Examples of removing functions from delegate chains can be found at o̲ᴄᴺ̲ⱽVB060009.

Can Delegates Be Used for Anything besides Callbacks?

Even though delegates are the mechanism behind callbacks in the .NET Framework, there is no stipulation that they be used solely for this purpose. Delegates can be useful in multicast/subscription situations, where the number of functions triggered by an event can change dynamically. See o̲ᴄᴺ̲ⱽVB060010 for an example that uses delegates in this manner.

SUMMARY

Delegates are used in the .NET Framework in place of callback functions, which were previously facilitated by VB's `AddressOf` operator. By acting as a buffer between functions and their callers, delegates can ensure that callbacks are performed in a type-safe manner. The ability of delegates to be used to wrap multiple functions allows for a phenomenon called *multicasting,* whereby one source notifies numerous functions of a given event.

Delegates are also the underlying mechanism behind events in VB.NET. With VB.NET, you still use the VB6 `events` and `Raisevents` keywords to expose and trigger events in your classes, but you must use the new `Handles` keyword to associate methods with events that classes raise. Behind the scenes, VB.NET translates your event statements into delegates, which are used to trigger events and invoke their event handlers.

Topic: Garbage Collection

One of the great features of Visual Basic 6 (and earlier versions) was automatic memory management by the VB Runtime. Unlike C and C++, whenever a variable is no longer being referenced, the VB Runtime destroys it and reclaims the memory it occupies. With VB.NET, it is the CLR that performs memory management, albeit in a slightly different fashion. To contrast the memory management characteristics of the VB Runtime with those of the CLR, consider the following block of VB6 code:

```
Public Sub MyRoutine
    Dim sC As SomeClass
```

```
    Set sC = New SomeClass() 'Remember, no Set in VB.NET

    'Rest of routine
End Sub
```

Listing 6.17   VB6 memory management example

After `MyRoutine()` has finished executing, the VB Runtime will correctly destroy the instance of `SomeClass` because it has gone out of scope. The behavior of the CLR is similar. At some point after `MyRoutine()` finishes, the CLR's garbage collector will determine that the `sC` variable is no longer being referenced and will destroy it. It is important to note the words "at some point" in the previous sentence—for the CLR does not guarantee *when* the garbage collector executes.

CONCEPTS

The Finalize() Method

Before we get into the nuances of garbage collection by the CLR, we must first examine a small syntax change in VB.NET. Visual Basic 4 gave developers the ability to write their own classes. By adding a class module to a project, you could author a class that exposed methods and properties to the rest of your application. If you wrote a class in VB6 that allocated resources, you were sure to release them in the class's `Class_Terminate` method. In VB.NET, you no longer use `Class_Terminate`, but place an object's cleanup code in its `Finalize()` method, as depicted in Listing 6.18.

```
Public Class SomeClass
    'Use Finalize instead of Class_Terminate
    Protected Overrides Sub Finalize()
        'If our object had allocated resources, it would
        'release them here.
    End Sub
End Class
```

Listing 6.18   The Finalize() method

You may wonder why we have used the `Overrides` keyword in the preceding code. Remember from our discussion of the Common Type System in Chapter 1 that all types in VB.NET derive from `System.Object`. One of the methods of `System.Object` is `Finalize()`. As we learned in Chapter 4, if we wish to replace an inherited class's method with our own, we must use the Overrides keyword, hence its inclusion in the Finalize() preceding declaration.

Nondeterministic Finalization

VB.NET's new Finalize() method is nothing more than a syntactical change from VB6. The real implications of garbage collection become apparent when we consider the following code, which illustrates when objects are destroyed by the CLR.

```
Public Class SomeClass
    Protected Overrides Sub Finalize()
        Console.WriteLine("SomeClass's Finalize() called.")
    End Sub
End Class


Module Module1

    Public Sub SomeRoutine()
        Dim sC As SomeClass
        sC = New SomeClass()
        'When this routine ends, myCS is no longer
        'being referenced and will be Garbage Collected.
    End Sub

    Sub Main()
        Dim k As Integer
        SomeRoutine()
        'The next time the CLR's garbage collector runs, it
        'will call Finalize() on SomeClass, interrupting our
        'loop of numbers below:
        For k = 1 To 10000
            Console.WriteLine("{0}", k)
        Next
    End Sub

End Module
```

Listing 6.19   The timing of garbage collection

The code in Listing 6.19 illustrates the unpredictable timing of the CLR's garbage collector. Let's analyze the Main() routine line by line. The second line in Main() calls the SomeRoutine() procedure. This routine creates an instance of SomeClass in the sC variable and then returns to Main(). Since sC has gone out of scope, it is no longer being referenced and must be destroyed the next time the CLR's garbage collector runs. In the meantime, `Main()` starts printing out numbers 1 to 10,000.

Add the code in Listing 6.19 to a Console Application project in VS.NET and call it GCollect. Build your application, then go to your project's bin directory from the command prompt (i.e., `\someDiectory\GCollect\bin\`). Run your application by executing the following line:

```
GCollect > numbers.txt
```

The preceding syntax may be unfamiliar to some developers. By appending `> numbers.txt` to our execution command, we are telling our application that any screen output is to be redirected to a file called `numbers.txt`. This technique is referred to as *piping* to a file. If you examine the `numbers.txt` file that was created (using a text editor such as Notepad), you will see that it contains a list of numbers. If you do a search for "Finalize" however, you will see something like the following:

```
..
4529
4530
SomeClass's Finalize() called.
4531
4532
..
```

Listing 6.20   GCollect's output

To understand what is happening, consider Listing 6.19 once again. After `Main()` calls `SomeRoutine()`, it begins outputting numbers to the screen (it really outputs them to `numbers.txt`, because we have piped the application's output). Remember, however, that the `sC` variable must still be garbage-collected. When the CLR's garbage collector runs, it calls the `sC.Finalize()` method, which interrupts the stream of numbers that `Main()` is printing. In the output in Listing 6.21, the `Finalize()` method interrupted `Main()` as it was printing number 4,530.

If you execute GCollect.exe numerous times and examine the `numbers.txt` file it produces, you will see that the CLR's garbage collector interrupts `Main()` at different points on each run (in five iterations we got values of 4,530, 3,632, 1,842, 8,406 and 2,964). This exercise demonstrates that you can never be certain when an unreferenced object will be destroyed—it all depends on when the CLR's garbage collector next executes. This unpredictable behavior is referred to as *nondeterministic finalization.*

Dispose() and SuppressFinalization()

Nondeterministic finalization may not seem particularly noteworthy. After all, what does it matter that an object is unnecessarily kept alive for some amount of time, as long as it is *eventually* destroyed? The answer is that objects that have allocated expensive resources (database connections, communication channels) must be able to release them in a more timely manner.

Microsoft's solution is to have classes expose a method that clients explicitly call when they are finished using objects. By placing cleanup code in this method as opposed to Finalize(), resources can be freed immediately and do not depend on the next execution of the garbage collector. Under the .NET Framework, the convention is to call this method Dispose(), although you can certainly name it something else (Close, Release, etc.). When we look at the Windows Forms classes in Chapter 7, we will see that many GUI classes must be released using Dispose().

The problem with this approach is that you are left in the precarious situation of hoping that clients call your Dispose() method. If they do not, expensive resources will never be freed, which can be as problematic as the original dilemma of having them freed in an untimely fashion. The solution to this problem requires using the SuppressFinalization() method found in the System.GC class. Under this approach, objects have two methods that free resources: Dispose() and Finalize(). Depending on the client's actions, resource release can proceed in one of two ways:

1. The client calls Dispose(). Dispose() releases the object's resources and calls GC.SuppressFinalization(), informing the CLR that Finalize() should not be called.
2. The client forgets to call Dispose(). When the object is garbage-collected, the CLR calls Finalize(), which releases the object's resources.

In the best case, a client calls Dispose() after using your object, and resources are immediately freed. In the worst case, a client forgets to call Dispose(), and the garbage collector eventually calls Finalize(). The following code demonstrates this hybrid approach:

```
Class SomeClass
    private Sub CleanUp
```

```
        'Cleanup resources here
    end sub


    public Sub Dispose()
        'Free resources:
        CleanUp()
        'No need for CLR to call Finalize, so don't let it:
        GC.SuppressFinalize(me)
    end sub


    protected overrides sub Finalize()
        'Client did not call Dispose!, free resources:
        CleanUp()
    end Sub
end Class
```

Listing 6.21   Dispose() and SuppressFinalize()

The GC.SuppressFinalize(me) line informs the CLR that the object has released its resources and that the CLR should not call Finalize(). As in VB6, the me construct in VB.NET refers to the current object instance on which the method is executing.

In addition to guarding against a client's failure to call Dispose(), you should also handle clients who might call your Dispose() method multiple times. In Listing 6.21, this would translate into determining whether resources have already been freed in the CleanUp() method.

Performance Issues

Keep in mind that you must implement Finalize() only if your objects require explicit notification of their destruction. If you implement Finalize() unnecessarily, you can significantly degrade performance. If a client instantiates a 5,000-element array of "finalizable" objects, for example, the CLR must call Finalize() explicitly against every element. Because of this, finalizable objects are typically destroyed later than their nonfinalizable counterparts. As a result of their demoted status, finalizable objects can unnecessarily prolong the destruction of other objects to which they have references.

Remember that you are not responsible for freeing other objects that your class may have instantiated. Consider object A that creates another object B. When object A is no longer being referenced, the CLR will garbage-collect it. Since A has been destroyed, object B no longer has any references (assuming A didn't share B with anyone), and it becomes a candidate for garbage collection. Upon the next run of the garbage collector, B will also be garbage-collected.

Thus, the CLR will eventually get around to destroying your objects and the objects to which they refer. Finalize() should be used only when an object has allocated expensive resources and it must free them in a more efficient manner.

HOW AND WHY

Can I Prevent an Object from Being Destroyed in its Finalize() Method?
The CLR garbage-collects objects when they are no longer being referenced. It is possible (although unlikely) for an object to establish a reference to itself in its own Finalize() method. This could involve setting some global variable to the object instance, as demonstrated by the following code:

```
protected overrides sub Finalize()
    someGlobalVariable = me
end Sub
```

As a result of this assignment, a reference to the object now exists, and it can no longer be collected. The object has thus gone through the unique cycle of being alive, being deemed OK to be destroyed (death), and being alive again. This fortunate change in the object's fate is called *resurrection*. Information on this advanced and rarely used technique can be found at ☜VB060010.

Is There a Way I Can Force the Garbage Collector
to Destroy Outstanding Objects?
Although the CLR will automatically run the garbage collector from time to time, you can run it explicitly by using the GC.Collect() method found in the runtime classes. However, you should be careful about forcing the garbage collector to run, as it will consume CPU cycles and may create unexpected pauses in your program. If you force the garbage collector to run too often, your application performance can seriously degrade, and you can quickly nullify any benefits derived from freeing the memory resources.

SUMMARY

Automatic memory management in VB.NET is now performed by the Common Language Runtime. Unlike the VB6 Runtime, which destroys objects immediately after they go out of scope, the CLR destroys objects by periodically running its garbage collector during program execution. There is thus a period of latency from when an object is no longer being referenced to when it is collected by the CLR. The duration of this period varies depending on when the CLR's garbage collector next executes.

Thus, while VB.NET objects can still receive explicit notification of their destruction by implementing the `Finalize()` method, they will often be left alive for an unnecessary period of time. This prolonged life span can undesirably delay the freeing of expensive resources that an object may have allocated.

Microsoft recommends that objects expose an additional method called `Dispose()`, which clients call once an object is no longer being used. This method, along with the `GC.SuppressFinalization()` method, means that object resource release proceeds in one of two ways. Either a client calls `Dispose()`, which releases the object's resources and calls `GC.SuppressFinalization()` so that `Finalize()` is not called, or a client does not call `Dispose()`and the CLR calls `Finalize()`when the object is garbage-collected.

Chapter Summary

In this chapter we examined some of the new language features in VB.NET. Attributes are declarative statements in your code that influence application behavior by embedding metadata into an assembly. An assembly's metadata can be retrieved using the programmatic technique of reflection, which can be used to dynamically invoke the methods of a class without prior knowledge of the class.

Delegates facilitate asynchronous notification between components and clients, and they are type-safe wrappers around functions. Because one delegate can wrap numerous functions (a chain), one component can call back numerous clients, a technique called *multicasting*. Delegates are also the mechanism behind VB.NET's event model, marking the end of the COM ConnectionPoint model that drove events in VB6. VB.NET introduces a new keyword called `Handles` that is used to specify which methods respond to a given event.

Like the VB6 Runtime, the CLR automatically manages memory for Visual Basic applications. Unlike the VB6 Runtime, unreferenced objects are not immediately destroyed but are garbage-collected sometime thereafter. Visual Basic classes no longer place their cleanup code in the `Class_Terminate` method but in the `Finalize()` method, which is called before an object is garbage-collected.

Chapter 7

—

WINDOWS FORMS

One aspect of Visual Basic that has remained remarkably consistent as the product has evolved is the VB Forms engine. As the underlying engine forms design in VB6, it can be argued that this entity alone is responsible for Visual Basic's widespread prominence. In this chapter we investigate VB.NET's replacement for the VB Forms engine, the Windows Forms Designer.

When Visual Basic was first released in 1992, its approach to application design was remarkably straightforward. Instead of the C++ technique, which required many lines of complicated code, VB allowed developers to paint their applications in an intuitive design environment. This approach was not only more intuitive than C++, but much faster as well. Even C++ purists couldn't help but be impressed by the fact that what took hours in C++ took minutes in VB. Although Visual Basic's capabilities now transcend simple GUI design, it is still arguably the standard choice for creating desktop applications for the Windows operating system.

For the first time in its history Visual Basic no longer comes packaged with the VB Forms engine. Instead, VB.NET (or, more accurately, the VS.NET IDE) contains the Windows Forms Designer (WFD). Application development with the WFD proceeds along the same intuitive lines as VB6—you paint applications and then associate event code with their various elements. The primary difference is one of abstraction; details that were hidden in previous versions of VB are now revealed by the WFD.

Windows Forms changes the properties of many intrinsic VB6 controls such as buttons, textboxes, and labels, all of which are now "classes" found in the System.Windows.Forms namespace. The second topic in this chapter discusses some of these changes, as well as some of the completely new features in the Windows Forms framework.

The first topic in the chapter clarifies how a control can now be a class, and our understanding of class inheritance from Chapter 4 allows us to investigate a completely new feature in the .NET Framework, called Visual Inheritance. Visual Inheritance is a technique that allows you to apply object inheritance principles to the GUI elements of your application. You can, for example, design a "base" form and then inherit its properties across multiple "derived" forms. As with standard class inheritance, changes to the base form automatically propagate to the derived ones.

The final topic in this chapter examines a technology called GDI+, a powerful graphics package that can be used for drawing shapes, filling surfaces with gradients and textures, and loading and manipulating images. GDI+ allows you to add impressive graphical elements to your VB.NET applications with relative ease.

Topic: The Windows Forms Designer

The Windows Form Designer is VB.NET's replacement for the VB6 Forms engine. To understand the role of WFD, we must first understand how its predecessor worked. When you create a GUI in VB6, the VB Forms engine does a lot of work behind the scenes. For example, the application shown in Figure 7.1 is very straightforward to create.

Figure 7.1   A simple application in VB6

Attach the appropriate code to the Command1 control in Figure 7.1 and you have a working application; the entire process would probably take you a few seconds. If we move this scenario to a language closer to the operating system (e.g., C/C++) things become a little more complex.

CONCEPTS

The Windows API

Recall from the first example in Chapter 5 that VB6 permits you to call Windows API functions. This powerful capability allows you to perform operations that cannot be done directly in VB6. The Windows API is the basis for all functionality in the Windows OS. Everything from printing to communications to GUI design is accomplished using the Windows API. Prior to the first version of Visual Basic (this was during the 16-bit the days of Windows 3.0) using the Windows API directly was the main option for creating applications.

The problem with the Windows API was that it is a C-style library. Intended for experienced developers, it had a steep learning curve and was cumbersome to use. If you wanted to change the color of a button, for example, you had to understand the idiosyncrasies of the various API functions you were calling. Furthermore, your design environment was not an intuitive form designer like VB6, but a text editor with many convoluted lines of code. The only way to confirm whether your code was correct was to compile and run the application. Through successive code changes and recompiles, the intended GUI would finally emerge.

The VB Forms Engine

If we were to write the application in Figure 7.1 using the C API, it would take us many lines of code. Today, this approach is almost never employed, thanks to the VB Forms engine, which, behind the scenes, takes care of all the complex API calls for us. These operations are buried somewhere inside the VB Runtime, but they are invoked every time a Visual Basic application executes. Thanks to the Forms engine, VB developers are largely abstracted from the Windows API that is implicitly called by their programs. While this is usually a blessing, it can be limiting in circumstances where one wants finer control.

It would be nice if VB exposed its underlying plumbing so we could, if we wanted, modify and build on it. That is, it would be nice if the VB Forms engine revealed the API calls it was making. VB.NET's replacement for the VB Forms engine—the Windows Forms Designer—does just that. The only difference is that the WFD doesn't make or reveal Windows API calls, but calls the classes found in the `System.Windows.Forms` namespace.

Creating applications using the Windows Forms Designer (WFD) is similar to previous versions of Visual Basic—you draw your application's graphical elements on a form and then write the event handlers behind them. When you draw a button, change its caption, change its size, the WFD translates your manipulations into VB.NET code that calls the Windows Forms classes. As the upcoming example will illustrate, this code is placed into a special region of the code listing that is marked with #region and #endregion tags.

Windows Forms Classes

The Windows Forms Classes can be found in the System.Windows.Forms namespace (this namespace is automatically referenced when you create a form-based application in VS.NET). The main class in this namespace is the Control class. Any component in the .NET Framework that has a GUI element must derive from this class, which handles user input and operating system notifications such as repaint requests. The Control class is at the top of the Windows Forms hierarchy depicted in Figure 7.2.

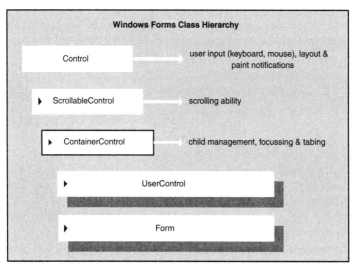

Figure 7.2   The Windows Forms class hierarchy

As can be seen in Figure 7.2, other controls in the Windows Forms framework extend the basic functionality of the Control class. ScrollableControl adds scrolling ability to a control, and ContainerControl gives a control the ability to house other controls by providing focusing and tabbing functionality. Two descendents of this class, UserControl and Form, are the ones you will interact with most often. The Form class is equivalent to a form in VB6 and is used to create Window screens and dialog boxes in VB.NET, and the UserControl class can be used to create your own custom controls.

The biggest challenge of Windows Forms is familiarizing yourself with the way many of these classes have changed from their VB6 counterparts. You cannot, for example, Unload() a form as you would in VB6. Instead, as we will see shortly, you must use a form's Close() method. The second topic of this chapter is dedicated to discussing many of these differences.

WINDOWS FORMS EXAMPLE

In this example we are going to re-create the application in Figure 7.1 using the Windows Form Designer. Begin by creating a Window Application project in VS.NET. After creating your project, VS.NET will bring up the design environment that we saw in Chapter 1, shown here in Figure 7.3.

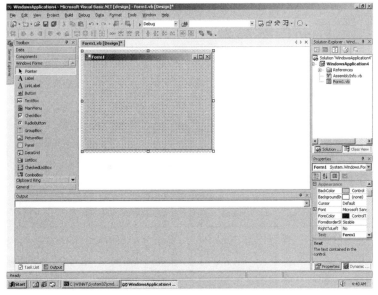

Figure 7.3   VS.NET design environment

Drag a button from the toolbox onto your form, and resize it so that you have something similar to Figure 7.4.

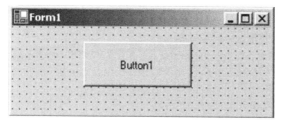

Figure 7.4   VB.NET application using the WFD

Double-click Button1 and insert the line `Me.Close()` so that you have the code shown in Figure 7.5 in front of you.

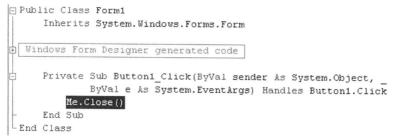

Figure 7.5   VB.NET application code

We have just written an application using the WFD, which is equivalent to the VB6 application in Figure 7.1. You can run the program by pressing F5 or going to the Debug menu and clicking Start. Look at the code in Figure 7.5, however, and you'll notice that it is considerably different from functionally equivalent VB6 code:

1. Instead of VB6's `Unload Me`, we used `Me.Close()` to close the form.
2. The method associated with the Button click's event (`Button1_Click`) is more complex than its VB6 equivalent. As we learned in Chapter 6, VB.NET's new event mechanism requires using the `Handles` keyword. The method also contains the `System.Object` and `System.EventArgs` arguments, which will be explained in a moment.
3. The event subroutine is called `Button1_Click` and not `Command1_Click` because the Windows Forms Designer gives Button controls the default name `Button1` as opposed to `Command1`, as in VB6.
4. Unlike Visual Basic 6, all of the code is contained in a class called `Form1`, which inherits from the `Windows.Froms.Form` class.

5. There is a curious boxed and grayed-out section, "Windows Forms Designer generated code."

Before we investigate exactly what the WFD is doing, let us first understand events handlers in VS.NET (item 2 in the preceding list).

WFD Event Handler

All events handlers generated by the Windows Forms Designer accept the following two parameters:

- `Object` This parameter represents the entity that invoked the event. Remember from Chapter 3 that everything in VB.NET derives from the `Object` type. Because anything could conceivably trigger an event, it makes sense to use a generic `Object` to represent it. In Figure 7.5, the entity that raises the `Button1_Click` method would probably be the button itself. Remember, however, that `Button1_Click` is just a normal method and therefore callable from other parts of our application. We may want to perform different actions depending on who invoked it. The following code displays a message box only if `Button1_Click` was invoked as a result of a button click:

```
Private Sub Button1_Click(ByVal sender As System.Object, _
    ByVal e As System.EventArgs) Handles Button1.Click

    If sender Is Button1 Then
        MsgBox("Event was triggered by Button1")
    Else
        MsgBox("Event was triggered by Someone else")
    End If

End Sub
```

- `System.EventArgs` The second parameter is a `System.EventArgs` class that contains information the event needs to communicate. In practice, event handlers that need to communicate information pass a class that *derives* from `System.EventArgs`. Because the `Click` event is very straightforward, it uses a generic `EventArgs` class. The `DateTimePicker` control we examine in the next topic, however, passes a more descriptive `DateTimeFormatEventArgs` class that can be queried for information.

Back to the WFD

The code in Figure 7.5 certainly looks different from the VB6 code you might be used to. When we created our project, VS.NET automatically created an empty form for us called Form1. Behind the scenes, the WFD created a class in our project called Form1 that inherits from the Form class in the System.Windows.Forms namespace. Remember that by inheriting from a class we automatically inherit any methods the class exposes. Thus, Form1 inherits methods such as Close(), Show(), and Refresh(), which are similar to those methods that a VB6 form exposes. It also inherits properties such as Size and Width, which define the dimensions of the form.

The role of the WFD isn't finished. When we added a button to the form, the WFD gave the Form1 class a private variable called Button1, which is an instance of the System.Windows.Forms.Button class. This may not seem obvious looking at the code in Figure 7.5, but you can see it if you expand the "Windows Forms Designer generated code" section as shown in Figure 7.6.

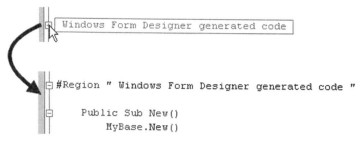

Figure 7.6   The WFD-generated code

If you expand the WFD section as shown in Figure 7.6, you will see that WFD-generated code is enclosed within #Region and #End Region tags. Scanning through this code (there is a lot of it), you will see the following two lines:

```
Private WithEvents Button1 As System.Windows.Forms.Button
...
Me.Button1 = New System.Windows
```

The first line declares the Button class, and the second instantiates it. Notice that the button is declared with the WithEvents keyword, allowing the button class to receive events from the form, such as mouse clicks. Look closely and you will see that the second line is contained in a private subroutine called InitializeComponent(). This subroutine is called from the form's New()method, which is similar to the

`Form_Initialize` method in VB6 (it is called before the form loads). The `New()` method is also contained in the WFD section that you expanded in Figure 7.6.

```
Public Sub New()
   MyBase.New()

   'This call is required by the Windows Forms Designer.
   InitializeComponent()
   'Add any initialization after the InitializeComponent() call

End Sub
```

Listing 7.1   The InitializeComponent routine

The `InitializeComponent()` method instantiates and configures all of the form's contained classes (buttons, labels, pictures, etc.). If you look in this method, for example, you will see the following lines that determine the button's size and location.

```
Me.Button1.Location = New System.Drawing.Point(90, 20)
Me.Button1.Size = New System.Drawing.Size(100, 50)
```

These line were generated by the WFD when you placed the button on the form. If you were to return to the form and resize the button, the WFD would change to second line of code to match your actions. Notice that a control's location and size are now specified using the `Location` and `Size` properties, although Windows Forms classes still expose the `Left`, `Top`, `Height`, and `Width` properties for backward compatibility.

You may be wondering if we can do the reverse. That is, can we change the underlying code and see a corresponding change in the button's size in the design environment? You can do this, but it is not advisable. The WFD doesn't expect you to modify the code it generates. If you make a change it doesn't understand—if you delete certain class declarations—it could damage your entire project file. For demonstration purposes, however, let's do something innocuous and change the first parameter in the button's `Size` property from 100 to 200. Return to the design environment and the button's width will have increased.

Look (but don't touch!) through the rest of WFD-generated code and you will begin to understand the intricacies of the Windows Forms classes. Examine the `Form1` class and you will note that it doesn't contain a `Close()` method. This may seem odd, given that we used this method in Figure 7.5 to close the form and terminate our application. Again, remember from Chapter 4 that by inheriting from the system's

Form class we automatically inherit its members. In addition to Close(), Form1 inherits other methods and events that VB6 developers would expect (Refresh(), Hide(), KeyDown, KeyPress, etc.).

Also remember from Chapter 4 that we can override a base class's methods using the Overrides keyword. If, for example, we wanted to write our own Refresh() method for Form1, we would do so as follows:

```
Public Overrides Sub Refresh()
   'Do our refresh (perhaps repaint some figures, etc)

   'Make sure we call Refresh on Form():
   MyBase.Refresh()
End Sub
```

Listing 7.2   Overriding a method

Listing 7.2 illustrates a very important rule when overriding methods of the Windows Forms classes: *be sure to call the base class's method you have overridden!* In the preceding code we replaced the Form's Refresh() method with our own implementation. However, the Form class we inherited from also has its own Refresh() code. It is extremely important, therefore, that we call Form's Refresh() method from within our own implementation using VB.NET's MyBase keyword. As its name suggests, this keyword can be used to invoke the methods of a base class from a derived class.

Experiment with some other controls in the VS.NET IDE (some of the newer ones are discussed in the next topic) and you will see that developing applications using Windows Forms is very similar to doing the same in VB6. The primary difference is that behind the scenes the WFD converts your actions into corresponding calls to the Windows Forms classes. The biggest challenge for developers will be getting used to the differences between the Windows Forms classes and the intrinsic controls in the previous version of VB (e.g., Close() versus Unload). The next topic in this chapter highlights many of these changes.

Windows Forms and Threads

As discussed in Chapter 4, VB.NET exposes threads that allow applications to have multiple streams of execution. If you are using threads in a form-based application, you must make special provisions, because *the Windows Forms classes are not thread-safe*. Essentially, this means that whenever a secondary thread (one that is spawned from the application's initial thread) attempts to access a Windows Forms class, it must do so using a special method called Invoke(). This method allows the CLR to synchronize access to the class. For an example of using the Invoke()

method, as well as a discussion on Windows Forms thread safety, please see ☞VB070001.

HOW AND WHY

Can I Use the Windows Forms Designer with Other Languages?
Remember from Chapter 5 that assemblies contain language-neutral IL code. The classes in the System.Windows.Forms namespace are no exception, and thus they are callable from languages such as C# and managed C++. To paint applications as you do in VB6, however, you need a tool such as the Windows Forms Designer that translates your graphical manipulations into code that calls the appropriate classes. As of this writing the WFD can generate code in VB.NET and C#.

This may have caught you off guard, but it means that you can also paint applications in C#. To try this, start a C# Windows application project in VS.NET. Instead of translating your actions into VB.NET code that calls Windows Forms classes, the WFD will generate C# code.

Note that if you wish to call the Windows Forms classes using languages other than VB.NET or C# (managed C++, for example), you must do so programmatically without the benefit of an intuitive design environment.

SUMMARY

The VB Forms engine that fueled application design in Visual Basic 6 has been replaced with the Windows Forms Designer in VB.NET. GUI development using the WFD is similar to VB6, which consists of pictorially designing your application and then associating event code with its elements. Behind the scenes, the WFD generates VB.NET code that calls the System.Windows.Forms classes. This code is placed in a special region of your code listing, denoted with the #region and #endregion tags.

The Windows Forms classes follow an object-oriented approach. A form with two buttons, for example, is really an inherited Form class with two private Button class variables. The characteristics of a GUI are represented through the properties these classes expose, such as Size and Location. Because they are really classes, the GUI elements in VB.NET applications are susceptible to classlike properties such as inheritance, which is covered in this chapter's Visual Inheritance topic.

Topic: Control Changes from VB6

The example in the previous topic demonstrated some of the differences between VB6 and VB.NET:

1. We had to use the form's Close() method instead of Unload to get the form to unload and terminate the application.
2. A control's size and location was specified using the Location and Size properties instead of the Left, Top, Height, and Width properties (although these older properties can still be used for backward compatibility).

Changes such as these—characteristic differences between intrinsic VB6 controls and their Windows Forms equivalents—will entail the biggest learning curve for developers. To this end, we present some of these critical changes here. Source code demonstrating many of these changes can be found at ⊶CN⟩VB070003.

1. Modal dialog boxes (dialogs that stay in front of an application until they are closed) are no longer displayed using VB6's vbModal parameter but must be displayed using a form's ShowDialog() method.
2. The Caption property for most controls has been replaced with the Text property. In Figure 7.4, if we wanted to change the Button's caption we would change its Text property from "Button1" to "Click Me."
3. In the VS.NET design environment, controls with no visible representation (such as timer controls) no longer appear on the form that contains them. Instead, they are placed on a separate pane underneath the form.
4. Controls no longer have HelpContextID and ToolTipText properties to provide online help and hints. In VB.NET, you must use the HelpProvider and ToolTip, controls which are Extended Provider Controls. When Extended Provider Controls are added to a form, they give all the controls on the form additional properties. If we were to add a ToolTip control called myToolTip to the application in Figure 7.4, for example, Button1 would now expose a property called "ToolTip on myToolTip". This property could then be used to display a tool tip when the user hovered over the button.

   Likewise, adding a HelpProvider control called myHelp would give Button1 the following properties to provide access to online help: `"HelpKeyword on myHelp"`, `"HelpString on myHelp"`, `"HelpNavigator of myHelp"`, and `"ShowHelp on myHelp"`.

5. As explained in Chapter 3, default properties have changed significantly under VB.NET. In VB6, for example, you can change the contents of a `TextBox` using the following:

```
Text1 = "Hello World"
```

Because `Text` is the default property of the VB6 `TextBox` control, the compiler knows that what you really mean is the following:

```
Text1.Text = "Hello World"
```

In VB.NET you *must* use the second variation.

6. VB6's `Frame` control has been replaced with the `GroupBox` and `Panel` controls. As with a frame, these controls can be used to encapsulate a number of other controls. Setting the `GroupBox.enable` property to `False`, for example, disables all the controls it contains. `GroupBox` and `Panel` can also be used to group a set of related controls, such as a collection of radio buttons. The major difference between the two controls is that a `Panel` can contain scrollbars to scroll through its viewable region.

7. VB6's `Image` control that is used to display images has been dropped in VS.NET. In previous versions of VB, the `Image` control was a lightweight version of the `PictureBox` control, consuming less memory because it could not be accessed outside the Visual Basic application that contained it (it didn't have a Window Handle). Now that most desktops have hundreds of megabytes of RAM, however, lightweight controls are often spurned in favor of more capable counterparts. As a result, you must use the `PictureBox` control to display images in the managed environment.

8. VB6 control arrays are not supported by the WFD. This is a significant exclusion that will make porting existing VB6 code to the managed environment more difficult. A control array is often useful because numerous controls can trigger the same event handler and allow the handler to determine the control that triggered it. You can obtain the same behavior in VB.NET by creating one method to handle the events raised by multiple controls. Examples illustrating this technique can be found at ⟐VB070004.

9. The menu editor found in VB6 is no longer used in VS.NET. To give a form a menu, you place a `MainMenu` control on a form, then edit the menu directly on the form. Behind the scenes, the WFD gives the form a `MainMenu` class, representing the entire menu, and `MenuItem` classes, representing each item in the menu (adding a menu to a form and inspecting the generated code is a good exercise).

   The `MenuItem` class exposes the `Checked` and `Enabled` properties that determine whether a specific menu item is checked or enabled, as well as the `Index`, `isParent`, `BarBreak`, and `Break` properties that determine the item's position in the menu. Remember that you can use the `MainMenu` and `MenuItem` classes programmatically as well. This means that you can dynamically add and remove items from a form's menu—something you could not easily do in VB6. An example demonstrating this can be found at ᴏᴄɴ⤳VB070005.

10. There are subtle differences when creating multiple document interface (MDI) forms in VS.NET. To add an MDI parent form to a VB.NET project, you do not use VB6's "add MDI Form" menu option, but set a form's `isMDIContainer` property to true. Similarly, to make a form an MDI child, you must use the form's `isMDIChild` property. There are also differences with respect to the controls an MDI parent form can contain, when a form can be designated a child, and so on. For details see ᴏᴄɴ⤳VB070006.

In addition to the preceding changes, the Windows Forms classes contain numerous features not found in VB6. Some of these are listed here, and a more complete reference can be found at ᴏᴄɴ⤳VB070007.

11. All VB.NET controls expose `Anchor` and `Dock` properties. With the `Anchor` property, you can specify that a control be kept a certain distance from a form's edges so that the control automatically resizes with the form. The `Dock` property is used to attach a control to one of the form's edges. Docking a control to the left edge of a form, for example, ensures that its distance from the form's left border is zero.

12. Forms now expose the `AddOwnedForm()` and `RemoveOwnedForm()` methods, which allow forms to own other forms. Forms that are owned are called *slave forms.* Slave forms are automatically minimized or closed with their masters. Additionally, slave forms always appear in front of their masters. An example of a slave form would be the spell checker of a word

processor that must always appear in front of a document and is automatically minimized with the application.

13. The ContextMenu class allows you to create pop-up menus that appear when a control is right-clicked. Referring to the application in Figure 7.4 again, you could give Button1 a pop-up menu by dragging a ContextMenu control onto the form called myPopUp. You would then edit the menu directly on the form and associate it with the button by setting Button1's ContextMenu property to myPopUp. Our next point gives a more practical use of ContextMenus.

14. A new control called NotifyIcon allows you to place icons in the Windows System Tray. This tray, which usually appears to the right of the Windows Task Bar, is often used to house background services such as antivirus and online messaging programs. The control's Icon property is used to determine the icon displayed. When you add this control to a form, the icon is automatically displayed in the System Tray when the application runs. This control is often used with a ContextMenu (discussed earlier), which can be used to display a menu such as the one shown in Figure 7.7 when the user right-clicks the icon in the System Tray. These two controls can help you write an application that runs in the background and is accessible via an icon in the Windows System Tray.

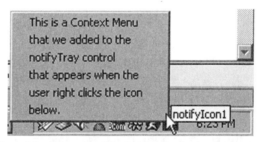

Figure 7.7   Associating a NotifyIcon control with a ContextMenu

15. Another new control called DateTimePicker offers a sophisticated method in which a user can select a given date. To get a feel for this simple yet powerful control, drag it onto a form and experiment with it. It is very similar to third-party ActiveX calendar controls for VB6, which makes selecting dates straightforward.

16. Rounding out the new classes in Windows Forms is the DataGrid control, which is a scrollable grid that can be bound to the ADO.NET DataSet that we examine in Chapter 9.

Changes in the underlying DataSet are automatically reflected in DataGrid and vice versa. For a DataGrid example consult ⌥VB070008.

SUMMARY

Visual Basic developers migrating to the .NET environment must familiarize themselves with the Windows Forms classes that replace the intrinsic controls used in VB6. These classes have changed significantly, exposing new properties, events, and methods.

There are also several new classes in Windows Forms that were not available in VB6. Examples include the NotifyTray, class used to add icons to the Windows System Tray, and the DataGrid class, used to manipulate ADO.NET Datasets. To produce quality desktop applications in VB.NET, developers must become comfortable with these new classes.

Topic: Visual Inheritance

Remember that controls in VB.NET such as textboxes, labels, and even forms are really classes found in the System.Windows.Forms namespace. As such, they are subject to the class inheritance properties illustrated in Chapter 4. You can develop a GUI in VB.NET and then inherit it in another project. When inheriting a GUI, you not only inherit its physical structure (control locations and sizes) but its associated code as well.

You have, in a sense, already used Visual Inheritance. Consider the application we created at the beginning of this chapter, depicted in Figure 7.4. When we created this project, the VS.NET IDE automatically created a form for us (called Form1) that inherited from the system Form class:

```
Public Class Form1
    Inherits System.Windows.Forms.Form
```

In this case, the inheritance was implicit—the Windows Forms Designer did it for us behind the scenes. If we wanted, we could instruct Form1 to inherit from some other form we created (say Form2). By doing this, Form1 would not only inherit the attributes of Form2 (its size, location, etc.), but would also inherit any controls it contained.

The most important aspect of Visual Inheritance is the accessibility of inherited controls. If Form1 inherits a button, for example, could we change its size and modify its event code? As we will see, this depends on the accessibility of the control in the inherited form (Form2). If the Button1 is private, then it is off limits—we can look but not touch. If it is public, then we can modify it in any way we desire. Visual Inheritance is best illustrated by the following example.

VISUAL INHERITANCE EXAMPLE

In this example we will create a simple GUI in one VB.NET project, then extend it in another. Complete source code for both projects can be found at ꝏVB070010. To begin, create a Visual Basic project in VS.NET. Instead of selecting the Windows Application template, however, select ClassLibrary and call your project BaseForm. A Class-Library is a DLL assembly, and exposes classes that can be used in other programs.

After selecting the ClassLibrary template, go to the Project menu, select Add Windows Forms, and call your form MyBaseForm. Resize the form and give it a button so that it resembles the form in Figure 7.4. Double-click the button and insert the following line of code, which is executed when the button is clicked:

```
Private Sub Button1_Click(ByVal sender As System.Object, _
   ByVal e As System.EventArgs) Handles Button1.Click
      MsgBox("myBaseClass code: Button1 was clicked")
End Sub
```

Listing 7.3   Event code for Button1

Compile the ClassLibrary by going to the Build menu and selecting Build Solution. You now have an Assembly DLL file that exposes the MyBaseForm class. You can verify this by using the ILDASM utility to inspect the Assembly, which is located in the \YourProjectDirectory\bin directory.

Remember, myBaseForm is simply a class that inherits from the System's Form class. Thus we can inherit myBaseForm itself in another VB.NET project. Save your project and create a new Windows Application project. VS.NET will automatically create an empty form for us called Form1. We will not use this form (we will create an inherited one momentarily), so right-click Form1.cs in the Solution Explorer window and select Exclude from Project. Now go to the Project menu and select Add Inherited Form. Call your form MyInheritedForm and click Open. VS.NET will now invoke a tool called the Inheritance Picker that will allow you to choose the form you wish to inherit from.

Click Browse and select the Assembly DLL that we previously created (remember, it is contained in the \YourProjectDirectory\bin directory). The Inheritance Picker will examine the Assembly and ask you to choose which form you wish to inherit from (see Figure 7.8).

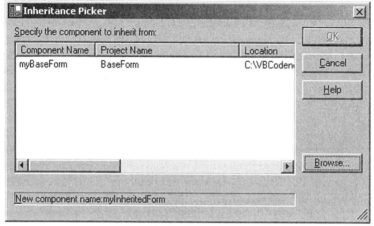

Figure 7.8   VS.NET's Inheritance Picker

Select MyBaseForm and click OK. VS.NET will now create a form called MyInheritedForm that inherits from myBaseForm. You can verify this by inspecting the underlying code generated by the WFD:

```
Public Class myInheritedForm Inherits BaseForm.myBaseForm
```

If you experiment with MyInheritedForm, you will find that you cannot resize Button1 or modify any of its properties (they will all be grayed out in the properties toolbox). If you attempt to click the button to attach event code to it, VS.NET will inform you that it is inaccessible by graying out its border (see Figure 7.9).

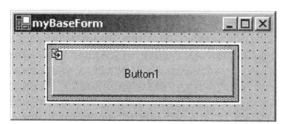

Figure 7.9   An inaccessible inherited control

This may seem like unusual behavior, but it makes sense if we examine the code for MyBaseForm. Open the ClassLibrary project you created, inspect the WFD-generated code, and you will see the following line:

```
Private WithEvents Button1 As System.Windows.Forms.Button
```

As can be seen, Button1 is a private member variable of MyBaseForm. It should come as no surprise, therefore, that it is off limits. Object-oriented principles tell us that although class inheritance inherits private member variables and methods, they are not accessible in the child class (MyInheritedForm, in our case). As such, Button1 is completely inaccessible in the design environment—we can't even attach event code to it. The only time the button is accessible is when the application runs.

Before we can run the application, there is one small step we must do. Right-click your project and select Properties. Click General and then select myInheritedForm under Startup *object*. Run the application by pressing F5, click Button1, and you will see the screen shown in Figure 7.10.

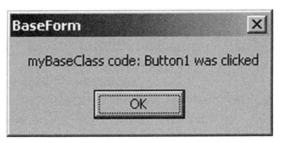

Figure 7.10   Inheriting MyBaseForm's code

As Figure 7.10 illustrates, we inherited not only the properties of myBaseForm but also its code. This should come as no surprise given what we learned in Chapter 4—class inheritance inherits structure and implementation.

If we wish to modify Button1 in the design environment, we must make it accessible in the base class by making it Public. Remember, however, that this line was generated by the WFD, and changing its code is not a good idea. A safer approach is to change the button's Modifiers property to Public using the property toolbox in the design environment. After doing this, rebuild the ClassLibrary and then reload myInheritedForm.

Notice that Button1 can now be resized, its properties changed, and event code added to it. You will notice that its properties are now accessible, and we can even attach event code to it. Double-click `Button1` and give it the following event code:

```
Private Sub Button1_Click(ByVal sender As System.Object, _
  ByVal e As System.EventArgs) Handles Button1.Click
    MsgBox("myBaseClass code: Button1 was clicked")
End Sub
```

Listing 7.4   Event code for Button1

If you the run application and click Button1, you will see two messages: the one in Figure 7.10 and one that contains the preceding message. Two messages result because both the base and derived class event handlers are called.

You may be wondering if you can suppress the base class's event code. That is, can we prevent the message in Figure 7.10 from being displayed? This is possible, provided that the base class's event handler for Button1 is `Public`. Look in Listing 7.3, however, and you will see that it is `Private`, so we are out of luck. The message in Figure 7.10 will always be displayed when the button is clicked. If the method were `Public` (if the base class author explicitly made it `Public` in Listing 7.3), we could suppress the message by *unregistering* the event handler. In Chapter 6, we learned that VB.NET uses delegates behind the scenes for events. To unregister an event, you must remove a function from the delegate chain. We demonstrate this approach at ᵒᴺ⟩VB070002.

The main point of Visual Inheritance is that the base class's author prescribes what can and cannot be done with the GUI. If you don't want a form's control to be modified, for example, set its `modifiers` property to `Private`. Likewise, for controls that can be modified, set their `modifiers` properties to `Public`. The `modifiers` property can also be set to `Assembly` or `Family`. `Assembly` makes the control accessible to only those entities within the same assembly, whereas `Family` makes it accessible only to the class and its decedents.

Visual Inheritance can be useful when you have a collection of forms that share common physical and functional characteristics. You could create a base form to embody these overlapping attributes, then have multiple child forms inherit from it. If one of these characteristics needs to be changed, such as renaming a common button or modifying its event code, you need only change the base form and the descendent classes will automatically inherit the modification. Also keep in mind that Visual Inheritance doesn't have to stop here. The descendent classes can in turn be inherited by other forms and so on. Any change in the base class would be reflected right down to the class hierarchy.

HOW AND WHY

Can I Inherit Forms Developed in Other Languages?

Chapter 5 demonstrated inheriting across languages. Because a form is really a class, the same principles apply here—you can inherit forms developed in C# or managed C++. Likewise, forms developed in VB.NET can be inherited by other languages.

SUMMARY

One of the most powerful aspects of Windows Forms is Visual Inheritance, which allows a form to inherit another form. When you inherit a form, you inherit its physical attributes, the controls it contains, and the code associated with the controls and the form itself. Visual Inheritance adheres to classic object-oriented principles—the ability to modify the members of an inherited class depends on their accessibility. If a form's button is `Private`, then it cannot be modified in the inherited form. If it is `Public`, then it can be modified. Using these rules, a developer can choose those portions of a GUI that can be changed when inherited and those that cannot.

Topic: GDI+

GDI+ is a powerful library that can be used to render graphics in your applications. Using the classes in the `System.Drawing` namespace, you can draw 2D graphics, perform image and font manipulation, and carry out sophisticated operations such as texture and gradient filling. GDI+ also includes native support for graphics formats such as JPG and GIF.

As its name suggests, GDI+ is an evolved version of the Windows Graphics Device Interface (GDI)—a subsection of the Windows API used to draw graphics and formatted text on video displays. GDI is a complex tool intended for C/C++ developers and requires you to familiarize yourself with low-level concepts such as device contexts, coordinate spaces, and graphic objects. Because of this, GDI is often spurned in favor of more intuitive frameworks such as the Microsoft Foundation Classes (MFC), OpenGL, and DirectX.

Given that GDI is a low-level graphics library, does it make sense to explore GDI+, given that VB6 developers had the majority of their graphics operations performed by the VB Runtime? As we will see, it does. In addition to providing very powerful graphical capabilities, a number of VB operations must now be done using GDI+. Consider the following VB code, for example, that draws a circle on a form:

```
Me.Circle (500, 500), 500
```

VB6 operations such as `Line()` and `Circle()` cannot be used with VB.NET—you must use the GDI+ alternatives (`DrawLine` and `DrawEllipse`) instead.

The GDI+ framework can be broken down into three subsections:

- **2D graphics**   These classes, found in the `System.Drawing` and `System.Drawing.Drawing2D` namespaces, are used to draw lines, ellipses, curves, and to fill surfaces with textures and gradients. There are also classes for matrix operations (used to transform images) as well as advanced image techniques such as alpha blending, which allows surfaces to behave translucently.
- **Image manipulation**   Contains classes that render and crop images in a variety of formats, including BMP, GIF, JPEG, EXIF, PNG, and TIFF. It also contains the `Metafile` class (not to be confused with `Metadata`) that allows a sequence of drawing routines to be recorded, saved to disk, and played at a later time. These classes are found in the `System.Drawing.Imaging` namespace.
- **Typography**   Includes classes to render fonts with special effects such as texture and gradient filling. These classes are found in the `System.Drawing.Text` namespace.

GDI+ is centered around the `Graphics` class, which represents a drawing surface such as a form or `PictureBox`. Those familiar with GDI can think of this class as the equivalent of a device context. You use this class to perform the majority of operations in GDI+, be it drawing an ellipse or rendering an image. Depending on the operation at hand, the `Graphics` class is used in conjunction with the following classes.

- **Brush**   The `Brush` class and its descendents (`SolidBrush`, `HatchBrush`, `LinearGradientBrush`) are used to fill a surface with colors, patterns, or even bitmaps. When calling `Graphics.FillRegion()` or `FillRectangle()` methods, for example, you must pass in the `Brush` used to fill the plane.
- **Pen**   The `Pen` class is used when a `Graphics` object draws lines, curves, and shapes using methods such as `DrawLine()`, `DrawCurve`, and `DrawEllipse()`. To draw a circle on a form for example, we would replace VB6's `Circle()` method with the following code:

```
Dim myGraphics As Graphics
Dim myPen As New Pen(Color.Black)
myGraphics = Me.CreateGraphics
myGraphics.DrawEllipse(myPen, 100, 100, 50, 50)
```

The CreateGraphics() method of a form returns a Graphics object representing the form's surface. Once we have obtained this object, we use its DrawEllipse() method to draw a circle (geometry review: a circle is really an ellipse with equal width and height). The ellipse is drawn with the Pen object we declared, in this case one that results in a ellipse whose outline is black. *It is important to note that when using GDI+, you specify coordinates using pixel values—not twip values as used in Visual Basic 6.* The second and third parameters of DrawEllipse() specify the center of the ellipse relative to the form, and the fourth and fifth parameters specify the ellipse's height and width.

• **Font** Use the Font class to describe the appearance of text you wish to render on the screen. You will most often use this class with Graphics. DrawString() method. The concept of "rendering text" may seem odd, until you realize that you can give fonts a gradient or textured background. You can also render a font by using *antialiasing* techniques, which gives it a smooth appearance, or by using Microsoft's ClearType font technology, which can improve a font's appearance on LCD screens. For details on GDI+'s font options, see ⊶VB070009.

GDI+ EXAMPLE

Visual Basic 6 developers rarely have to directly interface with GDI. One exception is when you want to create a form with irregular dimensions such as the one depicted in Figure 7.11.

Figure 7.11   An irregular form in VB6

You might use an elliptical form in a number of scenarios: for a splash screen, a tool-tip form that appears when a user scrolls over a certain control, and so forth. To create an irregularly shaped form in VB6, you constrain the viewable region of a normal, rectangular form to a shape you define. For an elliptical form, this involves using the GDI function `CreateEllipticRgn()` to create a virtual ellipse region and then applying it to the form using `SetWindowRgn()`. We will not reproduce the VB6 code here, but those interested can consult ⊕CNVB070011. The inescapable reality, however, is that you must use GDI to create irregular forms in Visual Basic 6, which is cumbersome and counterintuitive, given that the API caters to C and C++ programmers.

As we will see, doing the same task with GDI+ is straightforward, given the framework's object-oriented design. In the spirit of this example, we will give the VB application you created at the beginning of this chapter (Figure 7.4) an elliptical appearance.

To begin, bring up the VB application we developed in Figure 7.4. (If you haven't already done so, refer to the beginning of this chapter to create this project.) Use the property toolbox to change the form's `FormBorderStyle` to None, which removes its status bar and gives it a floating appearance. (See Figure 7.12.)

Next, add the following line to the top of the form's code to reference some of the classes we will be using. (Note that the VS.NET IDE will automatically reference the `System.Drawing` namespace.)

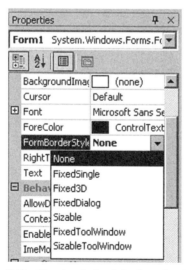

Figure 7.12   Changing the form's border style to None.

```
Imports System.Drawing.Drawing2D
```

Now add the following highlighted code to the form's New method (you have to open the Windows Form Designer's code to do this).

```
Public Sub New()
  MyBase.New()
  'This call is required by the Windows Form Designer.
  InitializeComponent()

  'Add any initialization after the InitializeComponent() call
  Dim gPath As GraphicsPath
  gPath = New GraphicsPath()
  gPath.AddEllipse(0, 0, Me.ClientSize.Width, Me.ClientSize.Height)
  Me.Region = New Region(gPath)
End Sub
```

Listing 7.5   GDI+ code to produce an irregular form

Remember that the form's New() method is similar to the Form_Initialize() subroutine in previous versions of Visual Basic—it is called before the form has loaded. Also note that whenever code is added to the New() method, *you must place it after the call to* InitializeComponent(). As we discovered at the beginning of this chapter, this method is generated by the WFD to initialize the form (i.e., to configure the form itself and to instantiate the controls it contains such as buttons and labels). Performing operations on a form before it has been properly initialized can have disastrous consequences (trying to resize a form's button, for example, before InitializeComponent() instantiated it would result in a NullReference exception).

The code we have added gives our form an elliptical appearance. To understand how it does this, we must define some GDI+ terminology:

- **Path**   Think of a path as a surface where lines and figures can be drawn. The path can be virtual, meaning it has no representation on screen, or it can represent a tangible surface that exists on a form, Picturebox, or any other GUI control.
- **Region**   A region specifies the permissible drawing area of a window.

The first two lines of our code declare a virtual path using the GraphicsPath object. The third line adds an ellipse to the path, whose height and width match that of the form. Remember, an ellipse isn't actually drawn on the screen—the path and its contents are an abstract representation in the computer's memory.

The final line does all the work. One of the properties of the `Control` class (remember from Figure 7.2 that the form class ultimately inherits from it) is `Region`, which specifies the viewable region of the control. The final line sets the viewable region of the form to the region defined by our virtual path, which consists of the single ellipse. The result is a form much like the one in Figure 7.11.

To demonstrate the additional prowess of GDI+, let's do something with it that you cannot do with GDI—let's give the form a gradient background. We do this by adding the following code to the form's class:

```
Protected Overrides Sub OnPaint(ByVal e As _
  Windows.Forms.PaintEventArgs)

  Dim myBrush As New LinearGradientBrush( _
    New Point(0, 0), New Point(200, 200), _
    Color.Black, Color.White)

  e.Graphics.FillRegion(myBrush, Me.Region)

End Sub
```

Listing 7.6   Giving our irregular form a gradient background

The `OnPaint` routine is similar to VB6's `Form_Paint` event that is called whenever the form is painted on the screen. Unlike `Form_Paint`, `OnPaint` supplies us with a `PaintEventArgs` class, which provides for us (among other things) the form's `Graphics` object that represents the form's surface. Using this `Graphics` object, we can modify the form's surface as we please (draw a line, draw an ellipse, etc.). In our case, we wish to fill its background. To do so, we need a brush object, and in our case we use a `LinearGradientBrush`. Similarly, we could have used a `SolidBrush` or `TextureBrush` to fill the form with a solid color or texture, respectively.

As a result of our efforts, the form now appears as shown in Figure 7.13 (when you build and run the application from the VS.NET environment, of course).

In our case, we specified that the gradient should fade from black to white—look at the third and fourth arguments in the `LinearGradient` declaration. The first two arguments specify the coordinates at which the

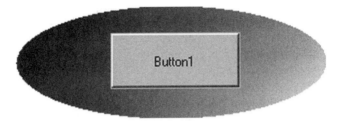

Figure 7.13   An irregular and gradient filled form

gradient begins and ends. Try playing around with different start and stop points, as well as different gradient colors using the Colors enumerations (Color.Blue, Color.Red, etc.).

Our example is but a survey of the numerous features in the GDI+ Framework, one that you are highly encouraged to explore. With its support for 2D graphics, typography, and image manipulation, colorful, attention-grabbing GUIs can quickly become a reality.

Before we depart GDI+, we must mention that GDI was also used to print documents. GDI+ inherits this capability. The classes found in the System.Drawing.Printing namespace (most notably the PrintDocument class) can be used to print documents. Visual Basic developers should note that these classes replace the Printer object that is used in VB6. For examples of the GDI+ printing classes, see ᵒᐧᶜᴺⱽVB070013.

SUMMARY

GDI+ is an evolution of the Graphics Device Interface (GDI) for the managed environment that allows you to draw 2D graphics and perform image and font manipulation. At the heart of GDI+ is the Graphics class that represents a drawing surface. This class is used in conjunction with the Brush, Pen, and Font classes to fill surfaces, draw shapes, and render text, respectively. In addition to these basic operations, GDI+ offers several advanced imaging techniques such as gradient and texture surface filling, antialiasing, and matrix operations.

Chapter Summary

Desktop applications in VB.NET are designed using Windows Forms, a set of classes in the System.Windows.Forms namespace that replace intrinsic VB6 controls such as textboxes, labels, and buttons. Using the Windows Forms classes is a transparent process, thanks to the Windows

Forms Designer (WFD), which allows you to create applications in VB6-like fashion. You still paint your applications, and behind the scenes the WFD produces VB.NET code to correspond to your actions. VB developers must familiarize themselves with the way these classes have changed from intrinsic VB6 controls; the `Frame` control, for example, must be replaced with either the `GroupBox` or `Panel` classes.

GUIs that are designed with Windows Forms can be visually inherited. Inheriting a GUI not only inherits its physical characteristics, but its code as well. Visual Inheritance adheres to the rules of object inheritance—if a base form's control is marked `Private`, then it cannot be modified in the inherited form, whereas if it is marked `Public`, then it can be modified.

Chapter 8

—

NATIVE CODE

Applications that you created with VB6 are considered *native* because they run outside the CLR. Similarly, external components that you use in VB6 such as Win32 DLLs and ActiveX controls are also of the native flavor. In this chapter we investigate the mechanisms .NET Framework exposes to call these native (sometimes referred to as *unmanaged*) components from VB.NET.

There are three types of native components that you might want to call from the .NET Framework:

1. **Win32 DLLs** Most often, you will want to call DLLs to access the Windows API. In Chapter 6, for example, we called the GlobalMemoryStatus() function found kernel32.dll.
2. **ActiveX/COM components** These are components that you access in VB6 using the Project → Reference menu option. Unlike ActiveX *controls,* components do not have visual elements. Examples include the ADO and DAO database libraries. ActiveX components are usually DLL files, although occasionally they are EXE files as well.
3. **ActiveX controls** These components are accessed in VB6 using the Project → Components menu option. ActiveX controls appear on the VB6 toolbar when they are selected, and they are usually OCX or DLL files. Examples include the WinSock control and Microsoft's Data Grid control.

Calling native components from the .NET Framework is undesirable. Remember that unlike VB.NET applications, native code executes outside the boundaries of the CLR. Invoking native components from within your VB.NET applications forces the CLR to suspend its execution and give way to code that operates outside its boundaries. This process is further compounded because the CLR must translate data between both sides of the fence using a process called *marshaling*. If you call a Windows API function that accepts a string, for example, the CLR must convert your managed System.String into an unmanaged equivalent and reverse the process when the function returns.

For performance reasons, it is good practice to avoid the use of native code where possible. The .NET Framework offers a strong set of features through the Base Class Libraries, which contains evolved versions of many technologies you have used in the past. As we will see in the next chapter, ADO.NET is a newer managed version of ADO.

That said, there are times when calling native code from VB.NET is unavoidable. Thousands of custom ActiveX controls exists for which there are no managed equivalents. Your company may have custom COM components that have not yet been ported to the .NET Framework. This chapter examines two technologies to call native code from VB.NET. Platform Invoke, or PInvoke for short, is used to call Win32 DLLs, and the COM Interop is used to call ActiveX controls and components. Leveraging both of these technologies is extremely straightforward using the VS.NET IDE.

Keep in mind that the techniques in this chapter are automatically utilized by the VB.NET Upgrade Wizard we examined in Chapter 3. If your VB6 project uses Win32 DLLs or ActiveX elements, the Upgrade Wizard will insert the necessary mechanisms into the converted VB.NET project. Nonetheless, this chapter will help you understand what the Upgrade Wizard is doing behind the scenes when it encounters native components in your VB6 applications.

Topic: DLLs and Platform Invoke

Platform Invoke is a technology to call Win32 DLLs from VB.NET. Most often, you will use PInvoke to leverage the Windows API. In Chapter 6, we called the GlobalMemoryStatus() function from VB6 by adding the following line of code to a module:

```
Public Declare Sub GlobalMemoryStatus Lib "kernel32" _
   (lpBuffer As MEMORYSTATUS)
```

As a result of this line, whenever we call GlobalMemoryStatus() from within our VB6 application the VB Runtime will load kernel32.dll and call the function appropriately.

Calling the Windows API from VB.NET is similar to doing the same in VB6. One difference is that we must use an attribute (covered in Chapter 6) called DllImport to specify where the function resides. This attribute is specified before the declaration of a function, as follows:

```
<DllImport("kernel32.dll")> _
Public Sub GlobalMemoryStatus(ByRef lpBuffer As MEMORYSTATUS)
      'Don't provide an implementation
End Sub
```

Listing 8.1   Using the DLLImport attribute

As with VB6, we can use GlobalMemoryStatus() as an intrinsic function in our VB.NET code. Because of the Dllimport attribute, the CLR knows it's an external API function and uses PInvoke to call it. There are a couple of caveats with PInvoke, however, as the following Console application demonstrates.

```
'We need the following line to use DllImport
Imports System.Runtime.InteropServices

'Use "Structure", not "TYPE" to declare
'a custom type (see Chapter 3)
Public Structure MEMORYSTATUS
    Dim dwLength As Integer
    Dim dwMemoryLoad As Integer
    Dim dwTotalPhys As Integer
    Dim dwAvailPhys As Integer
    Dim dwTotalPageFile As Integer
    Dim dwAvailPageFile As Integer
    Dim dwTotalVirtual As Integer
    Dim dwAvailVirtual As Integer
End Structure

Module Module1

    <DllImport("kernel32.dll")> _
```

```
Public Sub GlobalMemoryStatus(ByRef lpBuffer As MEMORYSTATUS)
End Sub

Sub Main()
    Dim mem As MEMORYSTATUS
    GlobalMemoryStatus(mem)

    'display amount of RAM on the system
    MsgBox(mem.dwTotalPhys)
End Sub
```

```
End Module
```

Listing 8.2   Calling the Windows API from VB.NET

Note from Listing 8.2 that we must `Import` the `System.Runtime .InteropServices` to access the `DllImport` attribute. If you compare the preceding VB.NET code with the VB6 code we wrote in Chapter 5 (Listings 5.1 and 5.2), you'll see a couple differences. First, note that we had to define the `MEMORYSTATUS` type using VB.NET's new `Structure` keyword (which we illustrated in Chapter 3).

Second, note that the fields in the `MEMORYSTATUS` structure are now all `Integers`, as opposed to `Longs` in our VB6 version (Listing 5.1). If you consult the data type table in Chapter 3 (Table 3.1), you will see that `Long` in VB6 is now `Integer` in VB.NET. This may seem like an unimportant detail, but if the fields in Listing 8.2 weren't converted, the program wouldn't function properly.

Remember, therefore, that when calling Windows API functions from the .NET Framework you must account for VB.NET's data type changes (the VB Upgrade Wizard will do this automatically when importing a VB6 application).

CONCEPTS

Aliasing
Aliasing is a technique to change the names of the DLL functions you are using. For example, in Listing 8.1 we may wish to call `GlobalMemoryStatus()` something else. Renaming the function is straightforward using `DLLImport`'s `Entrypoint` parameter:

```
<DllImport("kernel32.dll", Entrypoint="GlobalMemoryStatus")> _
Public Sub GetMem(ByRef lpBuffer As MEMORYSTATUS)
End Sub
```

Listing 8.3   DLLImport's Entrypoint parameter

As a result of the `Entrypoint` parameter, `DllImport` knows that `GetMem()` really maps to `GlobalMemoryStatus()` in `kernel32.dll`. We can now use the `GetMem()` function throughout our application.

Parameter Marshaling and Error Handling

`DLLImport` exposes additional parameters to control how the CLR marshals data and handles errors when calling DLL functions. Using `DLLImport`'s marshaling and error handling parameters requires low-level Win32/COM concepts such as BSTRs, HRESULTs, Unicode, and so forth. Using the `PreserveSig` parameter, for example, you could determine whether ActiveX errors manifest themselves as CLR exceptions or simply return explicit error code values that you must check. Such parameters are intended only for those developers who want fine-grained control over the CLR's native invocation mechanisms. For details on these attributes, as well as examples, please see o☜♥VB080001.

HOW AND WHY

How Do I Use Windows API Functions That Use Callbacks?

Many functions in the Windows API use callback functions. They accept a function address using VB's `AddressOf` operator and call this function to notify you that something has occurred. The `CopyFileEx()` function found in `kernel32.dll`, for example, will copy a file and call your function repeatedly after a certain number of bytes have been copied.

To call a Win32 function that uses a callback from VB.NET application, you must use the new type of callback mechanism in the .NET Framework called *delegates*. As explained in Chapter 6, delegates are type-safe and allow the CLR to properly move data between the managed and native domains. An example of using a delegate with the `CopyFileEx()` function can be found at o☜♥VB080002.

SUMMARY

To access DLL functions in VB.NET, you must use the `DllImport` attribute found in the `System.Runtime.InteropServices` namespace. This attribute is placed before the declaration of a function and allows you to specify the DLL the function resides in.

When a DLL function is called from VB.NET, the CLR must marshal its parameters and return values between the managed and native realms. The `DLLImport` exposes several parameters to assist the CLR in its conversion efforts and error handling characteristics. Information on these parameters can be found at ⟨CN⟩VB080001.

Topic: ActiveX and COM Interop

Using ActiveX controls and components from VB.NET is almost as simple as doing the same from VB6. Both entities can be accessed using menu options in the VS.NET's IDE and can then be used as if they were genuine .NET assemblies. As we will see, VS.NET must do a lot of work behind the scenes to facilitate such seamless interoperability. In this topic we will illustrate using both ActiveX components and controls from VB.NET.

CONCEPTS

Traditional ADO

As Chapter 9 illustrates, .NET offers a new version of ADO called ADO.NET, which is considerably different from its predecessor. Remember that calling native code from VB.NET incurs a performance hit, as the CLR must suspend its execution and marshal parameters to and from the native realm. Unless there is a compelling reason to use ADO, ADO.NET is the preferred choice of database access in the .NET Framework.

That said, we now demonstrate how to use traditional ADO from VB.NET. Begin by creating a Console project in the VS.NET. Next, go to the Project menu and select Add References. Click on the tab marked COM, and select the ADO library (version 2.5) as shown in Figure 8.1.

Click Select and then OK, at which point VS.NET will inform you that an Interop assembly must be generated. Click Yes, and VS.NET will do a lot of work behind the scenes to import our ActiveX component into VS.NET. After it completes its work, you'll notice that it has added a new reference to the project called ADODB (See Figure 8.2).

As illustrated in Figure 8.2, we now have a reference to the ADO library, which we can access through the ADODB namespace. A VB.NET program that utilizes ADO is almost equivalent to a VB6 program. The following program illustrates the minor differences.

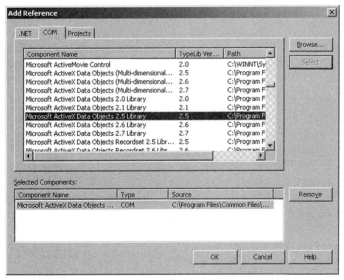

Figure 8.1   Using ADO in VB.NET

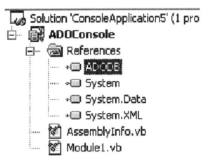

Figure 8.2   ADO reference in VS.NET

```
Imports ADODB

Module Module1

 Sub main()
    Dim mConnect As New Connection()
    Dim mRecord As New Recordset()
    Dim mCmd As New Command()

    'Open Connection (change to reflect you Database)
    mConnect.ConnectionString = ("driver={SQL Server};" _
```

```
    & "server=Poobong;uid=sa;pwd=;database=CodeNotes")

    'Obtain an ADO recordSet of the TradeTbl Table:
    mCmd.CommandText = "Select * From CompanyTbl"
    mCmd.ActiveConnection = mConnect 'No Set
    mRecord = mCmd.Execute   'No Set

    'Print all the StockIDs in the TradeTble Table
    mRecord.MoveNext()
    Do While Not mRecord.EOF
        Console.WriteLine(mRecord("StockSymb").Value)
        mRecord.MoveNext()
    Loop
    mConnect.Close()

  End Sub
End Module
```

Listing 8.4 A VB.NET program that uses ADO

The code in Listing 8.4 would be identical to VB6 code were it not for two syntax changes that we illustrated in Chapter 3:

1. The `Set` operator is no longer used to obtain new object instances.
2. Default properties are no longer supported in the traditional VB6 manner, which means we have to use the Recordset's `Value` property to obtain the `StockSymb` field.

Both these changes are bolded in Listing 8.4.

Interop Assemblies

Before we could use ADO in the previous example, VS.NET had to generate an interop assembly for us. An interop assembly is one that wraps the ActiveX component you are trying to use. For example, in Listing 8.4 our VB.NET application communicates with an assembly called ADODB. This assembly, in turn, communicates with the *real* ADO library. As you might imagine, there must be some type of buffer between the managed Interop assembly and the native ADO library. This entity is called a Runtime Callable Wrapper, or RCW for short.

Runtime Callable Wrappers

As we learned in the previous section, when the CLR calls a Win32 DLL, it must marshal parameters to and from the native world. Similarly, when the CLR uses a COM component, it must convert parameters into their proper COM representations. To do this, the CLR constructs an entity called a Runtime Callable Wrapper. In additional to marshaling responsibilities, the RCW must invoke the COM component and control the COM component's lifetime. The role of interop assemblies and the RCW are best understood if we consider the sequence of events that occur when Listing 8.4 is run:

1. VB.NET uses the ADODB interop assembly.
2. Because ADODB is an interop assembly, the CLR intercedes and determines which COM component it wraps (in this case, ADO).
3. The CLR constructs a Runtime Callable Wrapper and feeds it the appropriate information to instantiate the COM component.
4. The RCW instantiates the COM component (the ADO Library). The CLR can now call the RCW, which will redirect calls to ADO.
5. Any calls from the VB.NET application that use ADODB are redirected to the CLR.
6. The CLR redirects the application's calls to the RCW.
7. The RCW marshals parameters into COM equivalents and calls the ADO Library. The ADO Library does the appropriate work and then returns its results back to the RCW. The RCW converts the results into VB.NET managed types and returns them to the CLR.
8. The CLR returns the results to our application.

This may seem like a lot of steps just to call ADO! Thankfully, you don't have to worry about such details. VS.NET takes care of all the plumbing for you and makes the entire process transparent. Nevertheless, you can see why there is such a performance hit when you call native code from VB.NET. Three entities must work very hard to bridge the gap between the realm of the CLR and unmanaged ADO: the Interop assembly, the CLR itself, and the Runtime Callable Wrapper.

ADO/COM Interop Caveats

Although using ActiveX components in VB.NET is very straight-forward, there are a few things to watch out for. In Listing 8.4 we had to account for VB.NET's syntax changes before our code would compile. Additionally, you must account for a few behavioral changes that result when a COM component is converted into an interop assembly.

Consider the following line of code, which changes a Recordset's cursor type (the manner in which its records can be viewed):

```
myADORecord.CursorType = adOpenDynamic
```

This line, which compiles in VB6, will not compile under VB.NET. This is not a shortcoming of VB.NET, but a difference between the visibility of types in COM components versus .NET Assemblies. adOpenDynamic is part of the CursorType enumeration, and although the ADO COM component makes enumeration members globally visible to clients, assemblies require that you specify where they come from:

```
myADORecord.CursorType = CursorTypeEnum.adOpenDynamic
```

ActiveX Controls

Using ActiveX controls from VB.NET is as seamless as using ActiveX components in the previous example. Start by creating a Windows Application project in VS.NET. Right-click the Toolbox, select "Customize ToolBox," and then click the "COM Components Tab." Similarly to VB6, this dialog box allows you to choose the ActiveX controls you wish to use in your project. Choose one of them (try the Microsoft Winsock if it is on your system) and click OK. The control now appears in the toolbox, and it can be used like any other Windows Forms control in your project. (See Figure 8.3.)

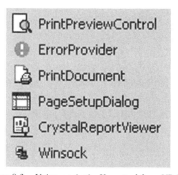

Figure 8.3   Using an ActiveX control from VB.NET

As with our previous ADO example, VS.NET must do a lot of work behind the scenes to facilitate communication with the unmanaged ActiveX control. It implicitly creates an interop assembly that communicates with the underlying ActiveX control. Interop assemblies that wrap ActiveX controls are prefixed with Ax. This is evident if you drag the Winsock control onto your application and look at your project's references (see Figure 8.4).

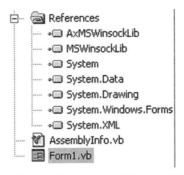

Figure 8.4   ActiveX interop assemblies end with "Ax"

HOW AND WHY

How Do I Use VB.NET Assemblies from VB6?

Just as you can use native code in VB.NET, you can use VB.NET assemblies from the native realm (VB6). To do this, you must use two utilities in the .NET Framework, called REGASM.EXE and TLBEXP.EXE. These utilities allow you to convert a .NET assembly into an ActiveX component so that it can be used in VB6.

Behind the scenes, the CLR constructs a COM Callable Wrapper (CCW). Like its RCW cousin, the CCW wraps an object across the CLR's boundary. The CCW also takes care of marshaling parameters between the two realms, as well as enforcing the security requirements of the assembly. For details on how to use REGASM.EXE and TLBEXP.EXE, please see ⌐CN⌐VB080003.

SUMMARY

Using ActiveX components and controls in VB.NET is very straightforward. To utilize an ActiveX component, you use VS.NET's Add References menu option and then select the component you wish to use. VS.NET will import the component into your project, and after referencing the appropriate namespace the component can be used like any other .NET assembly.

To use an ActiveX control, right-click on VS.NET's toolbar, select Customize Toolbar, and then select your control. The control will appear on VS.NET's toolbar and can now be used like any standard Windows Forms controls.

Behind the scenes, VS.NET creates interop assemblies to communicate between the managed world of the CLR and the native world of ActiveX. The interop assembly in turn uses a Runtime Callable Wrapper (RCW), which manages the underlying ActiveX component. Although these details are completely abstracted by VS.NET, they can significantly degrade performance due to the amount of overhead they involve. For this reason you should use native components sparingly and seek .NET equivalents where possible.

Chapter Summary

NATIVE CODE CAUTIONS

While many developers are likely to use the techniques in this chapter in order to call Win32 DLLs and ActiveX controls from the managed environment, caution must be taken when exercising this luxury. In Chapter 4 we discovered that the CLR uses lightweight AppDomains to house .NET applications.

Since a Win32 process houses multiple AppDomains (and thus multiple .NET applications), if your native code does something illegal (e.g., references an invalid pointer) it will destroy the entire process as well as any other .NET applications running within it. This behavior is in contrast to misbehaving managed code, whereby the CLR would just shut down the individual AppDomain.

In addition to the dangers associated with executing native code, a performance hit is incurred any time native code is called from the managed environment. For this reason, it is a good idea to reduce the number of transitions from the managed to unmanaged realms. If native functions are to be used, it is advantageous for them to perform many tasks and be called a few times, as opposed to performing a few tasks and being called many times.

Many developers reason that one of the advantages of native code over managed code is the superior performance of the former. While this may seem reasonable given that native code is not subject to the CLR's scrutiny, be careful when exercising this assumption, as the .NET Runtime has been highly optimized. We have encountered a number of cases where the Runtime equals or outperforms its unmanaged equivalent (see ᶜᴺ⟩VB080005). Even if native code performs slightly better, any speed gain can be easily nullified by the cost of transitioning to it in the first place.

WRAP-UP

The .NET Framework offers developers two choices to call native code from VB.NET. Platform Invocation (PInvoke) services allow functions residing in Win32 DLLs to be called using the DllImport attribute. This attribute is used to specify the DLL a function is located in so that the function can be used intrinsically in VB.NET.

VS.NET allows developers to use either ActiveX controls or components directly from its IDE. Behind the scenes, VS.NET constructs interop assemblies that wrap the ActiveX entity through the CLR's COM interop technology. COM interop technology is based on Runtime Callable Wrappers (RCW), which communicate between the managed world of the CLR and the native world of COM.

Chapter 9

—

A SURVEY OF .NET TECHNOLOGIES

.NET is more than simply a new version of Visual Basic. As we've seen in previous chapters, the framework introduces some fundamentally new concepts into Microsoft's computing methodology. In Chapter 1, for example, we saw that all code in the .NET Framework executes within the CLR, which is similar to a Java VM that interprets code before it runs. Chapter 5 examined the assembly, which solves the notorious DLL Hell problem through the CLR's use of public key cryptography.

The many changes in .NET are welcome additions to both Visual Basic and the operating system on which it runs, but the framework is more than simply an architectural fix for the Windows environment. To appreciate .NET's significance, we must venture outside the world of VB.NET and into the enterprise.

CORE CONCEPTS

History

The development landscape has changed dramatically over the past five years. One of the most significant innovations to have come about recently is the Java movement spearheaded by Sun Microsystems. Although the ideas of "open architecture," "write once, run on any operating system," and a "virtual machine that interprets code" have been around for some time, the meteoric rise of the Internet has created the critical mass necessary for these ideas to take root in mainstream development.

The first battle between Microsoft and Sun over compiled versus interpreted code was waged in the browser, where Microsoft countered Java by means of ActiveX. ActiveX is a traditional, compiled technology based on COM (Component Object Model). Whereas Java applets were downloaded to the browser and interpreted in real time by a Java Virtual Machine (VM), the compiled dynamic link libraries (DLLs) of ActiveX controls were downloaded to the client's file system by the browser, registered, and run as compiled code. The ActiveX strategy was, however, proprietary to Windows and Microsoft Internet Explorer. It can be argued that Java ultimately won this battle in that the binary ActiveX format is seldom used by major Internet sites, whereas Java applets are ubiquitous.

The second battle of technologies is occurring now, and it is happening not in the browser, but in the enterprise. The battlefield here is the server, the place where modern applications actually reside. In modern software architectures, we have moved to thin browser-based clients on the front end and on the back end a web server that shares the middle tier with some form of application server in which business logic is held.

One could say that for the past three years a war has been waged between Microsoft's application server, Microsoft Transaction Server (MTS), and Java's J2EE. MTS (COM+ on Windows 2000) houses components that you write, provided you compile them into machine code and adhere to the rules of COM. J2EE provides a means of doing the same thing (via something called Enterprise JavaBeans, or EJB), except that here there are many different vendors that provide application servers to house your components. MTS/COM+ runs only on Microsoft operating systems, but supports components written in multiple languages provided they follow the rules of COM. The J2EE/Application Server pairing will run on any platform, but the only language it allows is Java. No matter how theoretical the arguments, they boil down to compiled versus interpreted approaches. And so both camps stuck to their traditional strengths . . . until .NET.

.NET Services

With .NET, Microsoft is, in effect, abandoning its traditional stance in favor of compiled components and is embracing interpreted technology. With the introduction of the Common Language Runtime, Microsoft can offer a consistent set of enterprise services to anyone who utilizes its framework.

Not surprisingly, .NET was built from the ground up with the Internet in mind. XML is used throughout the framework as both a messaging instrument and for configuration files. An emerging communication protocol called SOAP allows components to interact (transfer data, perform RPC calls) via open Internet standards such as XML and HTTP. ADO.NET, Microsoft's new version of ADO, is based on a stateless and distributed access model, which is naturally suitable for web applications. Internet developers will also welcome WebForms (a part of ASP.NET), which brings the traditional ease and versatility of Visual Basic forms to Internet applications. Finally, .NET Remoting allows assemblies to seamlessly communicate over established protocols such as TCP/IP. In this chapter we will examine the various enterprise services in the .NET Framework.

Topic: ADO.NET

ADO.NET is the new data access model for the .NET Framework. ADO.NET is not simply the migration of the popular ADO model to the managed environment, but a completely new paradigm for data access and manipulation. ADO.NET was designed from the ground up with the distributed and stateless model of the Internet in mind. It was built upon the following two major design principles:

1. **Disconnected data**   In ADO.NET, virtually all data manipulation is done outside the context of an open database connection. Data is read into an entity called a Dataset, after which the database is immediately closed. Operations such as updates, inserts, and deletes are performed against the Dataset as required. When the database is ready to be updated, it is reopened and data is transferred from the Dataset. This model is appropriate for web applications, since they are not continually connected to their datastores.

2. **Universal data exchange via XML**   Datasets can be persisted and transmitted via the open XML standard. More specifically, a Dataset can save its contents to XML or import data in XML format. A significant limitation of traditional ADO was that it could be used only by COM-capable clients. Using standard XML, however, ADO.NET data can be easily transferred to non-Windows clients with no support for COM. This is especially important in the Internet's heterogeneous environment, where one may want to cooperate with non-Windows machines running Unix and the like.

With these principles in mind, we can divide the ADO.NET object model into two layers, the *managed provider*, which does the actual communication with the database, and the disconnected *dataset*, which stores the data.

CONCEPTS

Managed Providers

Managed providers are responsible for communicating with the database. Like the OLEDB and ODBC standards, the concept of a managed provider is not aimed at one particular database system. Instead, managed providers aim at exposing the common features of relational database systems via a simple programming interface. This is accomplished through the following four classes:

- **Connection**   Very similar to the ADO Connection object, used to establish a connection to a database.
- **Command**   Used to execute queries against the database.
- **DataReader**   Stores the results of a database query. The DataReader is a highly optimized forward-only, read-only method to examine data.
- **DataAdapter**   The mediator between the managed provider and the disconnected dataset. The DataAdapter uses Select, Insert, Update, and Delete commands to access and modify database contents.

At the heart of ADO.NET lies the Dataset object. Using the DataAdapter object, you populate a Dataset with relevant data. The database is then closed, and all data is temporarily stored in the Dataset. Changes to the Dataset (inserts, updates, deletes) do not persist against the database but are performed entirely in the Dataset's memory. The only time the underlying database changes is when you explicitly use a DataAdapter to update it. Based on the instructions from the Dataset, the DataAdapter will use the appropriate managed provider to force the required modifications to the given database.

The disconnected model just depicted is intended to be used by web applications that are intrinsically stateless. By performing the majority of data manipulations outside the context of open database connections, resources are saved and performance improves.

.NET ships with two optimized managed providers in the following namespaces:

- `System.Data.Oledb`   OLEDB managed provider
- `System.Data.SqlClient`   Managed provider for SQL server

Examples illustrating the use of ADO.NET's object model can be found at ⚬^{CN}VB090001.

Datasets

A `Dataset` is an in-memory representation of a database. Although it is tempting to think of the `Dataset` as the equivalent of an ADO `Recordset`, they are in fact very different. The ADO `Recordset` was centered around a single database table view. In contrast, a `Dataset` can contain multiple tables and the relationships between them. In addition, the `Dataset` can enforce relational constraints on the data it contains. Thus it is better to think of the `Dataset` as a lightweight in-memory database.

The previous section explained that a `DataAdapter` is used to populate a `Dataset` with data from a database. This is not, however, the only way a `Dataset` can obtain data. The power of a `Dataset` is its ability to obtain, store, and transmit data equally from a database or from XML. Data stored in a database is referred to as *relational data* because it is compartmentalized into tables and the relationships between them. On the other hand, data stored in XML is referred to as *hierarchical data,* based on a family tree structure (parent/child/sibling elements). Because `Datasets` can transfer data to and from either relational or hierarchical sources, developers are no longer restricted to using one model to represent their data.

The `Dataset`'s support for XML is also vital to sharing data in web applications. In practice, .NET web applications expose data as XML to clients, because you cannot assume which programming language the client was developed in or which platform it resides on. Using an open standard such as XML ensures that a vast range of clients will have access to data from .NET components.

A full discussion of the `Dataset` requires the introduction of topics such as strong typing, and XML relationships via schemas, and transactions, which are beyond the scope of this chapter. Articles and examples pertaining to these subjects can be found at ⚬^{CN}VB090002.

Topic: ASP.NET

ASP.NET is the next-generation Active Server Page (ASP) technology used to create distributed web applications. ASP.NET was developed to address some of the shortcomings of traditional ASP and to incorporate many new features web developers have long desired. This topic will briefly describe the major features of ASP.NET, including support for fully compiled languages, separation of code from content, Web Controls, and intuitive GUI design. For those familiar with ASP, a more detailed dissection of the differences between ASP and ASP.NET can be obtained at ⌐ᴺ⟩VB090004.

Support for Compiled Languages

One of the downfalls of ASP was that it supported only scripting languages. These languages, such as JavaScript or VBScript, typically provide only a subset of the functionality exposed by complete development environments such as Java or Visual Basic. Another shortcoming is that scripting languages are weakly typed, meaning that all variables are Variants, or generic types. This often results in error-prone code, because no type checking is performed at design time.

ASP.NET aims to bring the power of traditional desktop applications to the Web. One way ASP.NET realizes this is by adding support for fully compiled languages. Instead of using VBScript, ASP.NET allows you to use the full VB.NET language. This gives web developers access to traditionally unavailable features such as strong typing and object-oriented programming.

Separation of Code from Content

If you have ever worked with ASP, you are probably familiar with the awkwardness of mixing HTML with script code. This often results in unmanageable code, both in length and style, commonly referred to as *spaghetti code.* ASP.NET solves this issue by defining a clear separation between the HTML interface and the .NET assemblies that encapsulate business logic. Not only does this result in more maintainable code, it also allows for design and development teams to work together more seamlessly on web applications.

Web Controls

Following object-oriented design principles, ASP.NET pages make use of server-side controls called *web controls.* These controls, which are full-fledged objects, reside completely on the server. When a web application is loaded, it determines the capabilities of the requesting client browser. Web controls then render themselves on the client as standard HTML or DHTML (if supported by the browser). Since web controls reside on the server and render themselves as pure HTML, clients can access ASP.NET pages without any knowledge of the .NET Framework. Furthermore, because the capabilities of a browser are automatically determined, advanced browsers receive advanced functionality (frames,

DHTML, etc.), while more primitive browsers are still able to access the application.

ASP.NET ships with a wide variety of web controls that encapsulate functionality that previously would have required a large amount of HTML and script code to implement. They fall under the following categories:

- **Intrinsic controls**   These web controls essentially wrap standard HTML elements in objects (HTML textboxes and buttons).
- **Rich controls**   ASP.NET currently ships with two rich controls, namely the AdRotator (to display banner ads on a page) and a calendar control. Rich controls are meant to encapsulate advanced HTML user interfaces and script code in a convenient web object.
- **Validation controls**   ASP.NET ships with a host of web controls that simplify the process of validating user input. For instance, controls are available that ensure a field contains a value, fits a range of values, or matches a regular expression. In addition, the developer is given the option of linking a validation control to a custom server-side function. The power of these controls is their ability to be used in combination to provide flexible input validation. For more information and examples of validation controls, please refer to ⟳VB090003.
- **List and data controls**   These web controls provide flexible ways to display data in an itemized list. Controls range from a simple `Repeater` (essentially a basic read-only list) to an extensive editable `DataGrid` control. A detailed description of list and data controls and their application can be found at ⟳VB090005.

ASP.NET also provides a robust set of features for binding database or XML data to virtually any ASP.NET user-interface control. This feature, referred to as *data binding,* is discussed in detail at ⟳VB090006.

Intuitive GUI Design
Thanks to VS.NET, ASP.NET web interfaces can be designed with the same ease as VB6 forms. A tutorial on using the IDE to rapidly develop user interfaces can be found at ⟳VB090007.

Web Application Configuration
One of the big problems with ASP was the difficulty associated with configuring a web application. Application configuration was stored primarily in an entity called the IIS metabase, which was very difficult to move to a separate machine. ASP.NET resolves this issue by moving all

application configuration into flexible XML configuration files. An understanding of configuration files is important for properly deploying a web application. Examples and reference material can be obtained at ⟨CN⟩VB090008.

Topic: .NET Web Services

Web services are software components that expose themselves through the open Internet standards HTTP and XML. Applications running on remote machines on potentially different platforms can access these components in a language-independent manner. This topic presents a conceptual overview of web services. A technical overview with examples can be found at ⟨CN⟩VB090009.

CONCEPTS

Fundamentals

Web services usually run under the auspices of Microsoft's Internet Information Server (IIS). Like ASP.NET pages, web services are written with fully compiled .NET languages such as VB.NET and C#. The only difference between a regular .NET component and a web service is that certain methods are marked as *web-callable*. This means that clients have the ability to access these methods over the Internet.

When a service is requested by a client, IIS takes care of instantiating the web service component and invoking the requested method. Web services do not maintain state in between method invocations. This means that each call to the web service results in a new component being instantiated. Class-level private variables therefore do not persist in between method invocations. Thus, web services are typically used in situations where a finite amount of work is done, after which the component is no longer required. For example, a component that determines and returns the current price of a stock could be implemented as a web service.

Web services are advantageous because they can be accessed anywhere by anyone who understands HTTP and XML. Since messages to and from a service travel over HTTP, web services are not hindered by firewalls. This is especially important for corporations who wish to expose extensive business logic to clients on the web, but do not wish to compromise the security of their networks.

WSDL

In order for clients to use a web service, a description of the methods and types exposed by the service, along with the calling convention, must be readily available. Web services publish their exposed methods and types via a document written in an XML grammar known as *Web Service Description Language* (WSDL).

Upon request, IIS automatically generates the WSDL document for a given web service. Understanding the structure of a WSDL document is important when developing clients that utilize the service. A detailed look into the structure of a WSDL document is available at ∘ᶜᴺᵧVB090010.

Consuming Web Services

Having determined the method exposed by a web service using WSDL, a client would then invoke it. Recall that web services are available to clients via HTTP and XML. There are actually three methods of communicating with a web service, namely, HTTP GET, HTTP POST, and SOAP. The difference between these three protocols lies in how parameters are passed to the web service. In the case of HTTP GET and HTTP POST, web service method parameters are passed as name-value pairs (e.g., x=0, y=1). With SOAP (Simple Access Object Protocol), on the other hand, parameters are passed as an XML document embedded in the HTTP message.

The advantage of a SOAP request is that you can describe complex data types (such as ADO.NET datasets) instead of simple name-value pairs. Of course, the added flexibility comes at the cost of performance. Because XML is much more verbose than name-value pairs, SOAP messages take longer to transmit and interpret than do HTTP GET/POST messages.

Remember, only HTTP and XML are required to call a web service. Clients can range from a web browser to a Visual Basic 6 application. Examples of different clients that access a sample web service can be obtained at ∘ᶜᴺᵧVB090011.

Web Service Discovery

Remember that WSDL files describe the methods and types exposed by a web service. If a company wishes to deploy a web service for access to the general public, there must be some way for clients to locate and obtain the WSDL document. This is accomplished with another type of XML document known as a Web Service Discovery (or DISCO) file.

When clients request a DISCO file for a certain web site, IIS dynamically determines the web services available on the site. IIS then returns the DISCO file to the client, which points to all of the appropriate

WSDL documents. The DISCO file can be used to create a client that appropriately calls and interprets the results from a web service. Details on DISCO, along with case studies on web service applications, are available at o🔗VB090013.

Topic: .NET Remoting

.NET Remoting allows objects in different AppDomains, be they on the same or different machines, to communicate with one another. Recall from Chapter 6 that an AppDomain is the managed environment created by the CLR to house a .NET application. The Remoting Framework provides a flexible set of services to simplify the process of creating, instantiating, hosting, and interacting with remote objects.

Conceptually, .NET Remoting is very similar to the Web Services Framework—both allow you to communicate with a remote object. The difference is the amount of flexibility at the hands of the developer. Whereas web services stipulate that objects must reside in the IIS and must communicate using HTTP, Remoting does not enforce these restrictions.

Remoting objects do not have to be placed under the scrutiny of a bulky web server such as IIS, nor do they have to adhere to one communication protocol. The added flexibility, however, comes at the cost of complexity. .NET Remoting can quickly delve into the difficult concepts of object lifetime, leasing, and Remoting contexts that are beyond the scope of this book. A more extensive overview of Remoting, with applied examples, can be found at o🔗VB090017.

CONCEPTS

Proxies

.NET Remoting is based on the concept of a proxy object. When your client application uses a remote object (one on a different machine), it does not talk directly with the component. Instead, it talks to a proxy object, which ferries calls to the real object. Through this illusion, the proxy acts as a mediator between client and server, encapsulating all of the logic required to package and transmit messages between the two entities.

The mechanism a proxy uses to communicate with a remote object is called a *channel*. Recall that web services communicate with clients using XML over HTTP—better known as SOAP. Remoting gives the developer more latitude in defining the communication mechanism. For instance, developers can choose from the following communication protocols supported by the .NET Framework:

1. **HTTP**   Similar to web services. Messages between client and server proceed as standard HTTP, in most cases over port 80. This is good for cases where a firewall separates the client from the server. (Recall that firewalls do not block standard HTTP messages.)
2. **TCP**   In cases where firewalls are not of concern, the TCP channel offers greater performance.

You can further customize the process of communication by selecting the *formatter* used to encode/decode messages to and from remote object. The .NET Framework comes with two standard formatters that go hand in hand with the standard channels:

1. **SOAP**   Data is transmitted as XML payloads in HTTP messages. For more information on SOAP, please see ⌐CN⌐VB090015.
2. **Binary**   Data is packed into a compact (albeit proprietary) binary stream.

By default, the HTTP channel uses the SOAP formatter to encode and decode messages to and from the remote object. The higher-performance TCP channel, on the other hand, uses the binary formatter by default. Note that .NET Remoting is designed in an extensible way to allow third parties to customize or design their own channels and formatters. More information on this procedure can be obtained at ⌐CN⌐VB090016.

Remoting

Recall that web service components do not maintain state in between method invocations. Each time a client calls the web service, it is instantiated, used, and destroyed. .NET Remoting is considerably more versatile. Depending on your requirements, a remote object can be configured in one of three ways:

1. **Single call**   The remote object is instantiated for the sole purpose of responding to one request (from one specific client), after which the object is deallocated.
2. **Singleton**   The remote object is instantiated to server requests from various clients.
3. **Client-activated objects**   As the name suggests, this remote

object is instantiated upon request from a client. Client-activated objects remain dedicated to one specific client.

Configuring a remote object as a single-call object makes sense if the object is required by a client to do a certain amount of work, after which the object is no longer required. For example, a single-call object may calculate and return an interest rate. A singleton object, on the other hand, is used in cases where multiple clients speak with the same remote object and share data between one another. A singleton server object may, for example, serve as a chat engine. Finally, *client-activated objects* serve well when a single client needs access to the remote object but repeatedly calls methods on the object. In this case, keeping the remote object alive for several requests reduces the overhead associated with component instantiation.

Hosting a Remote Object

After you have decided on the configuration of a remote object (single call, singleton, or client activated), as well as the communication channel to be used, the next step is to host the remote object on a server. Recall that web services are hosted by IIS. When a SOAP request arrives for a service, IIS takes care of instantiating and directing method calls to the proper .NET component. Remoting components can also be hosted in IIS. On machines without IIS, however, you can also host a remote object in a standard .NET executable. In either case, all that is required is an AppDomain in which the component resides. Also, the developer must register the remote component with the Remoting Framework using Remoting configuration files. For details, please see ⟨CN⟩VB090016.

Chapter Summary

The .NET Framework is not simply a new environment for Visual Basic, but is Microsoft's aggressive strategy for both enterprise and personal software development. By prescribing that all .NET applications run within the CLR, the .NET Framework can offer a consistent set of enterprise tools through the Base Class Libraries.

ADO.NET is Microsoft's new version of ADO and is based on the disconnected model for web applications that are intrinsically stateless. Microsoft's new version of ASP, called ASP.NET, brings the traditional ease and versatility of Visual Basic forms to Internet applications.

Two services in the .NET Framework allow clients to remotely communicate with objects. Web services expose objects through the open Internet standards of XML and HTTP. Web service objects are instantiated every time they are called and are therefore stateless. .NET Remoting allows clients to communicate with objects using more specialized communication mechanisms such as TCP/IP. Remoting objects can maintain state and can be used in areas where web services HTTP overhead may be substantial.

Index